UNLOCKING THE POWER OF SMALL BUSINESSES

Indian Entrepreneurship
Legacy, Ecosystem, Opportunities

Perumal Koshy

Contents

Page. No

Foreword

Once considered a "fifth wheel in the process of development of capitalism, small enterprises, of late, have come to the centre- stage of development agenda in many countries. Way back from the 1940s itself, visionaries like Mahatma Gandhi and Schumacher came up with an articulation of the role of the small enterprise constituency, the rather late realization in most of the advanced capitalist countries is because of a much different rationale. In fact, today, in the practice of enterprise priming by public promotional agencies in many countries, the actual intentions often remain under the carpet. It is against this backdrop that this book by P.Koshy, a long- time practitioner in the subject area, becomes relevant.

Koshy's SME story, running through 20 chapters, comes out with the politics and social reality around the growth and transition of small enterprise sector in India's diversified industrial structure. Starting from the story of its legacy-induced roots that dates back to the Indus valley civilisation, the discussion goes along India's 'Freedom Movement', where 'khadi', the political wheel, emerged at a time as the symbol of rural employment, and a vision for running the economy. At a time when the small industry role was considered residual and transitory, especially by USA and UK, India developed its own model of small enterprise- based development, which subsequently got integrated with the Mahalnobis Model, to build up the country's edifice of modern industrialisation. While entrepreneurship was traditionally associated with 'business houses' in India, affirmative action for entrepreneurship development gradually developed into the culture and practice; it now adorns a proud of place in education and training .

The book makes an excursion into the thinking and practice in modern times with special reference to ideas such as creativity, co-creation, design thinking, multi culturalism, circular economy, renewable energy etc., moves forward with a discussion on the Fourth industrial Revolution. Lack of a comprehensive understanding of the SME constituency and of entrepreneurship in their totality, is a major hurdle in policy and practice today. While program priming is vital for realising the objectives of SME policy in the country, there exist limited and partial understanding of these two inter-related constituencies, even with financial institutions and promotional agencies.

As a practitioner, I have noticed a real need for a realistic India story of how the enterprise system works, "against the festive drum and far-heard clarinet of "of the so-called global "Development" rhetoric. The book stands out in terms of its implied intellectual provess in making things simple and intelligible to the common men. The authors need to be complimented for making this book an easy reading for all who are interested in the SME and Entrepreneurship role in the Indian economy.

P.M.Mathew
Senior Fellow& Director
Institute of Small Enterprises and Development

Preface

From the bustling spice routes of the Indus Valley civilization to the groundbreaking tech startups of today, India boasts a rich and enduring legacy of entrepreneurship. This spirit, a vibrant tapestry woven from millennia of history, unwavering resilience, and boundless innovation, is the very essence of what makes India's economic landscape so dynamic.

"Unlocking the Power of Small Businesses: Indian Enterprise, Legacy, and Ecosystem" delves deep into the heart of this phenomenon. The book embarks on a captivating journey, exploring the historical roots that laid the foundation for this thriving ecosystem. It uncovers how India's entrepreneurial heritage is deeply entrenched in its cottage industries, traditional village enterprises, and the very bedrock of the nation – its agricultural sector.

Entrepreneurship in India is more than a historical footnote. It is a lifeblood, a vibrant ecosystem where risk-taking, creativity, and a relentless pursuit of opportunity take center stage. This book dissects the intricate network of stakeholders, resources, and institutions that collectively support and facilitate the growth of entrepreneurs and businesses. This interconnected web, known as the entrepreneurship ecosystem, is fueled by a shared set of values: a willingness to push boundaries, a belief in the power of human ingenuity, and an unwavering commitment to progress.Understanding and nurturing this ecosystem is crucial for fostering innovation, economic development, and job creation. The book equips readers with the knowledge to navigate this dynamic landscape, whether they are seasoned business leaders seeking to adapt or budding entrepreneurs with a vision for the future.

The journey continues by witnessing the transformation of India's economic landscape through the lens of history. It explores the pivotal role of the 1991 economic reforms, a turning point that ushered in an era of liberalization, privatization, and globalization, paving the way for a wave of new opportunities.

Innovation, however, is not a solitary pursuit. The book delves into the power of design thinking, a human-centric approach that empowers entrepreneurs to create solutions that not only meet customer needs but also contribute to a sustainable future. It explores the unique strengths of multicultural entrepreneurship, where diverse backgrounds are harnessed to fuel creativity and build successful ventures with a global perspective. The book does not shy away from the challenges either. As it navigates the complexities of the Fourth Industrial Revolution, it explores the opportunities and hurdles faced by small and medium enterprises (SMEs) in this rapidly evolving technological landscape. The focus remains firmly on the future. The book unlocks the immense potential of emerging sectors like sustainable agriculture, renewable energy, and digital initiatives. By aligning ventures with these key areas, entrepreneurs can not only drive economic growth but also empower communities and promote environmentally responsible practices.

Readers will encounter inspiring stories and cases of individuals who dared to dream and build. Their journeys are testaments to the enduring power of the Indian entrepreneurial spirit.
This book is more than just a historical narrative or a business manual; it is a roadmap to success. Whether readers are brimming with innovative ideas or seeking to refine their existing business strategies, the practical insights gleaned from these pages will equip them to thrive in the dynamic world of entrepreneurship.

Acknowledgements

The successful completion of this book would not have been possible without the invaluable contributions and support of several individuals and organizations. Heartfelt gratitude is extended to Dr. P. M. Mathew, Director of ISED, for providing the insightful foreword that sets the tone for this book.

I am grateful to Dr. Antal Szabó, Scientific Director, ERENET, Hungary, for his encouragement, which inspired me to contribute research articles and essays focusing on entrepreneurship and small enterprise policy.

Special thanks are extended to Vighnesh Jha, Amar Singh, Bhavesh Jha, Jatin Pokhriyal, Mansi Gaud and C.K Vishwanath for their unwavering support at various levels. My heartfelt gratitude goes to Anita for her meticulous editing and proofreading, which significantly enhanced the readability and coherence of this book. Their collective insights, encouragement, and dedication have greatly contributed to the depth and breadth of this book, and their support is sincerely appreciated.

May the enduring flame of Indian innovation guide every reader on their entrepreneurial journey.

Perumal Koshy

"The future depends on what you do today."
- Mahatma Gandhi

"India's entrepreneurial spirit, rooted in resilience and innovation, has the power to shape the future and create a legacy of progress."
- Ratan Tata

1

India's Entrepreneurial Renaissance

The legacy of Indian entrepreneurial ecosystem dates back to the Indus Valley of 3300 BC, with a robust trade history and entrepreneurial culture.

India boasts of a rich entrepreneurial heritage deeply entrenched in its cottage industries, traditional village enterprises, and the agricultural sector.

India boasts a rich entrepreneurial heritage deeply entrenched in its cottage industries, traditional village enterprises, and the agricultural sector. Regrettably, during the colonial era under British rule, entrepreneurial roots were severely weakened.

The legacy of Indian entrepreneurial ecosystem dates back to the Indus Valley of 3300 BC, with a robust trade history and entrepreneurial culture. Trade and business ties have existed with different parts of the world at various points in time since then. The presence on global trading routes such as the Silk Route and maritime spice trade is well documented.

- The seeds of India's entrepreneurial spirit were sown much earlier than many realize.
- Indus Valley (3300-1300 BC): Evidence suggests vibrant trade with Mesopotamia, Persia,

and Central Asia, facilitated by well-developed land and maritime routes.
- Skilled artisans produced high-quality goods like textiles, pottery, and jewelry, prized for their durability and beauty.
- Planned cities, standardized weights and measures, and sophisticated drainage systems showcase a keen entrepreneurial spirit.
- Trade flourished along the Silk Road, linking India with China, Rome, and beyond.
- Indian merchants dominated the maritime spice trade for centuries, exporting valuable commodities like pepper, cloves, and ginger.
- Trade fostered the exchange of ideas, technologies, and products, shaping India's diverse cultural landscape.

India possesses a rich entrepreneurial culture deeply rooted in its cottage industries, traditional village enterprises, and agricultural sector. Unfortunately, during the British Raj, India's entrepreneurial foundation was severely undermined. However, the freedom movement sparked a renewed focus on revitalizing the village economy and nurturing entrepreneurship, symbolized by the emphasis on the Charkha and self-reliance.

In the post-independence period, economic policies predominantly centered on public sector undertakings, entailing stringent governmental oversight and an overwhelming regulatory framework.

This period, an era of "License and Permit Raj", called by Rajaji, was marked by exhaustive inspections and the prerequisite of licenses and permits for almost every facet of business operations.

LICENSE RAJ

The term "License Raj," coined by Chakravarti Rajagopalachari, describes a system where the Indian government had a lot of control and regulations over the economy from the 1950s to the early 1990s. Under this system, businesses needed government licenses and permits to operate at every level and point, and getting these licenses and permits were often a difficult and complicated process. Within this framework, Indian businesses were obligated to secure government licenses to conduct their

operations, and the acquisition of these licenses were often a challenging and arduous process. It required private companies to satisfy numerous government agencies—sometimes up to 80—before they could start producing things. Even after getting a license, the government continued to regulate production. Rajagopalachari believed that the License Raj could lead to political corruption and economic stagnation. He was so concerned about this that he founded the

Swatantra Party to oppose these practices.He believed in encouraging competition and protecting workers' rights while also limiting the role of government in certain industries. He opposed government interference in trade and the bureaucracy that came with it.Over a period of time the economy emerged with lots of control over businesses, entrepreneurs and private sector. Rent seeking officials and bureaucrats and rampant corruption in the industrial administrative system prevailed and grew.

2

Entrepreneurial Culture

Entrepreneurial culture is the lifeblood of innovation and progress. It's a vibrant ecosystem where risk-taking, creativity, and opportunity thrive, fueled by a shared set of values and a supportive environment. Entrepreneurial culture is a set of shared values, beliefs, and behaviours that encourage and support entrepreneurship.

Entrepreneurial culture is a set of shared values, beliefs, and behaviors that encourage and support entrepreneurship.

Entrepreneurial culture is more than just a buzzword; it represents a dynamic and influential force within societies, communities, national economies, and organizations. It encapsulates a set of shared values, beliefs, and behaviors that not only endorse but actively promote entrepreneurship. This way of thinking is characterized by a deep appreciation for innovation, a tolerance for risk, and a commitment to creating new opportunities.

It is a way of thinking and a culture that is prevalent in a society, community, national economy, or organization, valuing innovation, risk-taking, and the creation of new opportunities.

At the societal level, entrepreneurial culture is a prevailing force that shapes the way communities and nations approach economic development. When a society embraces entrepreneurship, it fosters an environment where individuals are encouraged to think creatively, take risks, and explore uncharted territories. This cultural foundation is vital for cultivating a positive atmosphere that supports entrepreneurs in their journey towards creating and realizing innovative ideas.

Youth Empowerment and Risk-Taking.
A positive approach and an encouraging atmosphere for entrepreneurs.

Central to entrepreneurial culture is its reflection in the support and encouragement of youth experimenting with risk-taking behavior to create opportunities and spur innovation. By instilling a sense of empowerment and resilience, entrepreneurial culture inspires the younger generation to break free from conventional paths and explore the world of possibilities that entrepreneurship offers.

Media's Role in Nurturing Businesses.
Reflection in the media supporting businesses, particularly small entrepreneurs, artisans, craftspeople, and micro, small, and medium-sized enterprises.

Entrepreneurial culture finds expression in the media's role in championing businesses, especially those led by small entrepreneurs, artisans, craftspeople, and micro, small, and medium-sized enterprises (MSMEs). A robust entrepreneurial culture encourages media outlets to highlight success stories, provide insights into the challenges faced by entrepreneurs, and actively contribute to creating a supportive ecosystem for burgeoning businesses.

Government Support and Policies. An encouraging approach to entrepreneurship should come from government agencies.

For entrepreneurial culture to thrive, it requires an encouraging approach from government agencies. Policymakers play a crucial role in creating an environment that fosters entrepreneurship through supportive regulations, financial incentives, and initiatives that empower entrepreneurs at all levels. A government committed to fostering an entrepreneurial culture recognizes the role small businesses play in economic development and actively works towards their growth and sustainability.

Educational Institutions and Academia. Educational institutions and academia generally encourage youth to pursue entrepreneurial behaviors rather than becoming job seeker.

Another key aspect of entrepreneurial culture is its influence on educational institutions and academia. Rather than emphasizing traditional career paths, educational institutions increasingly promote entrepreneurial behaviors among students. The goal is to nurture a mindset that values innovation, critical thinking, and problem-solving, preparing students to become creators and leaders in their chosen fields.

Entrepreneurial culture is a powerful force that permeates through society, influencing the way individuals, communities, and nations approach economic growth and development.

By fostering a mindset that values innovation, risk-taking, and the creation of new opportunities, entrepreneurial culture empowers individuals to break free from conventional paths and explore the limitless possibilities that entrepreneurship offers.

A vibrant entrepreneurial culture benefits everyone, not just entrepreneurs. It leads to new jobs, economic growth, and a more innovative and responsive society.

Building a thriving entrepreneurial culture is a long-term commitment, but the rewards are significant. By nurturing a supportive environment, encouraging risk-taking and innovation, and providing the necessary resources, we can empower individuals to turn their ideas into reality and create a more dynamic and prosperous future for all.

3

Entrepreneurship, Enterprise and Enterprise Ecosystem

The entrepreneurship and enterprise ecosystem refers to the interconnected network of various elements that collectively support and facilitate the growth and success of entrepreneurs and businesses. It encompasses a wide range of stakeholders, resources, institutions, and factors that contribute to the overall environment in which entrepreneurship thrives. Understanding and nurturing this ecosystem is crucial for fostering innovation, economic development, and job creation.

Entrepreneurship is the process of starting and running a business. It involves taking risks, innovating, and creating value for customers. Entrepreneurs are driven by a desire to be their own boss and make a difference in the world.

Enterprise is a business organization and are typically for-profit businesses, but they can also be non-profit organizations or government agencies. They are characterized by their complex structures, hierarchical management, and focus on long-term growth.Enterprise ecosystem is the network of interconnected actors, resources, and institutions that support entrepreneurship and enterprise growth. This includes things like universities, incubators, investors, accelerators, mentors, and professional services providers. A thriving enterprise ecosystem provides entrepreneurs with the support they need to succeed.

- Entrepreneurship is the engine that drives enterprise growth.
- Enterprises are the products of entrepreneurship.
- Enterprise ecosystems provide the fuel and support that entrepreneurs need to succeed.

A healthy and vibrant enterprise ecosystem is essential for economic growth and development. It creates jobs, generates wealth, and fosters innovation. By supporting entrepreneurs and enterprises, we can create a more prosperous and sustainable future for all.

ENTREPRENEURSHIP, ENTERPRISE AND ENTERPRISE ECOSYSTEM

A healthy and vibrant enterprise ecosystem is essential for economic growth and development. It creates jobs, generates wealth, and fosters innovation. By supporting entrepreneurs and enterprises, we can create a more prosperous and sustainable future for all.

Entrepreneurship is the engine that drives enterprise growth.

Enterprises are the products of entrepreneurship.

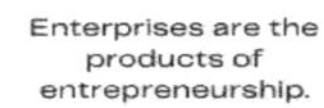

Enterprise ecosystems provide the fuel and support that entrepreneurs need to succeed.

Risk-taking, innovation, value creation

Entrepreneurship
The process of starting and running a business

Enterprise

A business organization

Complex structure, hierarchical management, long-term growth

Enterprise ecosystem

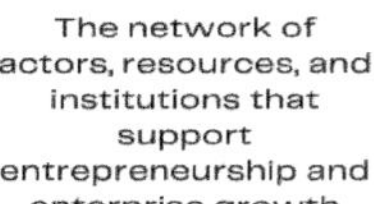

Universities, incubators, investors, accelerators, mentors, professional services providers

The network of actors, resources, and institutions that support entrepreneurship and enterprise growth

The objective of an effective enterprise eco-system and entrepreneurship policy is the creation of a conducive climate nurturing entrepreneurship. Central to this objective is the establishment of a comprehensive framework designed to equip, encourage, and educate prospective entrepreneurs with the requisite proficiencies to initiate and effectively steer their ventures.

Entrepreneurial ecosystem help describe the conditions that bring people 'together, foster economic prosperity towards wealth creation' by way of entrepreneurship, innovation and new venture creation.

Elements of Entrepreneurship ecosystem

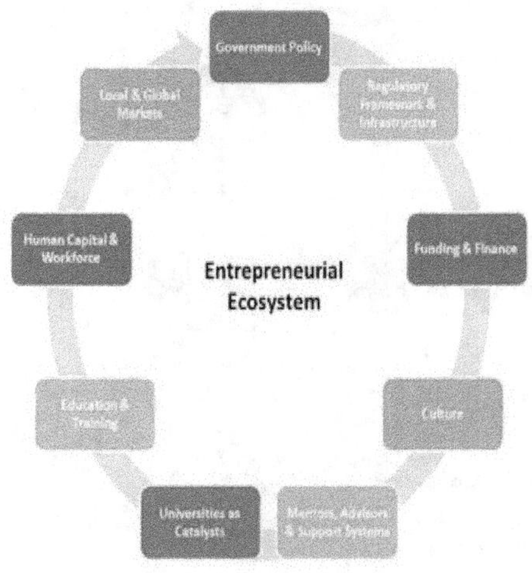

*Leela's Journey in Sustainable Farming,
Organic Ghee Production, and Overcoming
Market Challenges*

*Leela's Cow farm and Organic Ghee Venture Lee-
la, a resilient widow from Kerala, India, embodies
the spirit of entrepreneurialism against all odds. She
shoulders the responsibility of her family, including
three children — one in college and two with disabili-
ties Entrepreneurship, Gender, Diversity and Innovation — and runs a small organic farm focused on
dairy production. Leela's story holds valuable lessons
for sustainable living, resourcefulness, and navigating the challenges of rural entrepreneurship in
India. Resourceful & Sustainable: Leela harnesses
the abundant grass from uncultivated paddy fields
near her home, significantly reducing dependence on
expensive cattle feed.*

This not only lowers costs but also contributes to the unique quality of her milk and dairy products. Organic & High-Quality: Leela's small farm is entirely organic, resulting in milk with exceptional quality, health benefits, and a delightful flavor. Her grass-fed cow's ghee, known for its distinct taste and aroma, is particularly sought after by non-resident Indians (NRIs). Market Value Gap: Unfortunately, Leela is unaware of the premium value her organic, grass-fed ghee could command.

Online platforms like Amazon India and Flip-kart sell similar products for INR 950- 1000 per 500 grams, significantly higher than the local price of INR 300 she receives. Market Access & Fair Pricing: Despite her commitment to organic practices and quality, Leela faces challenges in accessing broader markets and obtaining fair prices for her products. Leela's case is a unique to many women owned business, which hints at factors that are common to women owned ventures which restrict their growth.

Despite strides in educational attainment at primary and secondary levels, gender gaps persist in the critical skills necessary for running a successful enterprise. While women have made significant progress, they often lack the combination of education, vocational and technical skills, and work experience essential for developing highly productive businesses.

Note: Adapted from "Unlocking Farmer Prosperity: Strategies for Multiplying Income and Strengthening Market Linkages, Global SME News, 4 July 2023, https://globalsmenews.com/unlocking-farmer-prosperity-strategies-for-multiplying-income-and-strengthening-market-linkages/

4

Entrepreneurship Policy and Evolution

India's entrepreneurial eco-system, evolved over several centuries. From the ancient traders who established maritime routes to the modern tech startups disrupting industries, the Indian entrepreneurial ecosystem has constantly evolved and adapted to changing times.

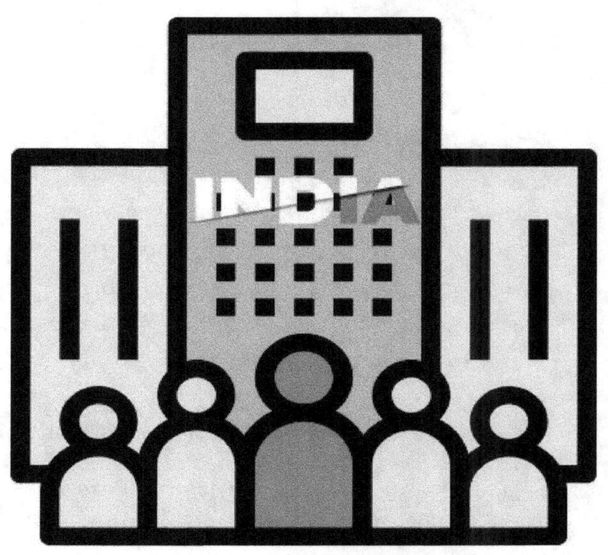

India's earliest entrepreneurial ventures were driven by trade and commerce. Merchants established trading links with countries across Asia, Europe, and Africa, exporting spices, textiles, and other goods.

India has a long tradition of craftsmanship, with skilled artisans producing exquisite textiles, jewelry, and other products. These industries were often family-run businesses, passed down from generation to generation.

The British Raj imposed restrictions on Indian businesses, limiting their growth and development. However, some Indian entrepreneurs managed to find success in sectors such as textiles, tea, and jute.

The Indian independence movement saw a surge in entrepreneurial activity, as Indians sought to build their own businesses and reduce dependence on British goods.

After independence, the Indian government initially focused on building a strong public sector. However, in the 1990s, the economy was liberalized, opening up new opportunities for private businesses. Since the liberalization, India has seen a boom in private enterprises, with new startups emerging in sectors such as IT, pharmaceuticals, and e-commerce. oday, India's entrepreneurial ecosystem is supported by a growing network of incubators, accelerators, and investors. The government has also launched several initiatives to promote entrepreneurship, such as Startup India.

Despite the progress made, India's entrepreneurial ecosystem still faces challenges, such as access to finance, complex regulations, and lack of skilled manpower.

Gandhiji identified the collapse of textile economy as fundamental to the economic devastation caused by East India Company and the British Raj. He directed the Congress to include constructive work to village industries.

Features of traditional enterprise eco-system:

- Production for the need of the region/ village
- Sustainable use of resources
- Principle of conservation in the use of products & manufacturing
- Role of castes/communities in manufacturing and delivery of various services
- Cottage/home based manufacturing
- Labor intensive techniques
- Finance by rural money lenders
- Caste and community in determining enterprise focus

Mixed economic system during the post-independence era, resulted in the emergence of public sector units along with the private sector. Enterprise policy was embedded in the industrial policy resolutions (Industrial policy resolution , 1948). After the adoption of the constitution, the Industrial Policy was comprehensively revised and adopted in 1956.

To meet new challenges, from time to time, it was modified through statements in 1973, 1977 and 1980 (DC SSI, n.d.), which outlined the approach to industrial growth and development.

In 1991 the government adopted economic reforms and a new industrial policy (GoI, 1991), which accorded enhance priority for small enterprises, easing of regulatory burden and creating a single window approach to licenses, permits and clearances emerged as important policy focus, which led to the way towards an entrepreneurial ecosystem that promotes a favorable entrepreneurship culture (Panagariya, 2004; Koshy, December 2019).

Industrial development and Entrepreneurship policies in the post independent pre liberalized era

Some Highlights

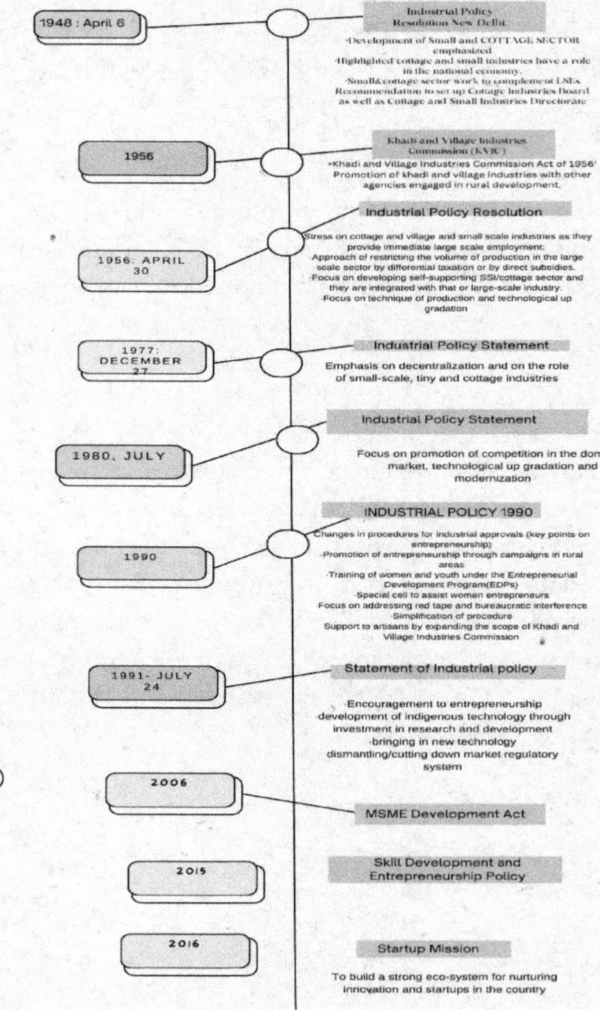

5

Creativity, Innovation, and Entrepreneurship.

Creativity is the characteristic of someone or some process that forms something novel and of value. The created item may be intangible (such as an idea, a scientific theory, a musical composition, or a joke) or a physical object (such as an invention, a printed literary work, or a painting).Innovation is the process of implementing new ideas and solutions into the real world to create value. Combining creativity and innovation can lead to groundbreaking solutions, like self-driving cars or personalized medicine, that can profoundly change the game for businesses. Creative problem-solving can help in identifying new opportunities and developing innovative new products or services.

Creativity is a characteristic of someone or some process that forms something new and valuable. The created item may be intangible (such as an idea, a scientific theory, a musical composition, or a joke) or a physical object (such as an invention, a printed literary work, or a painting). Creativity is about generating ideas and thinking outside the box. Innovation is about implementing those creative ideas to create tangible and valuable outcomes.

Creativity can be described as the ability to generate novel and valuable ideas, solutions, or expressions. It involves thinking divergently, making unique connections, and approaching problems in innovative ways.

How will you generate new ideas and solutions?

- Creativity is the ability to generate new and valuable ideas.
- Innovation is the process of applying creative ideas to produce tangible and beneficial outcomes.
- Entrepreneurship is the act of recognizing and capitalizing on innovative opportunities for business success.
- Entrepreneurs play a crucial role in the innovation ecosystem by recognizing the market potential of creative ideas and taking the necessary steps to bring them to fruition.

- Successful entrepreneurship often involves a combination of creativity, strategic thinking, and the ability to turn innovative concepts into viable and sustainable ventures.
- This process contributes to economic development, job creation, and the overall advancement of society.

Everything revolves around creativity. All industries, new developments, changes, collapses, strategies, designs—everything revolves around creativity, creative thinking, and creators.

Creativity as Currency

In a rapidly evolving world where new challenges and opportunities continually emerge, creativity acts as a valuable currency.

Creators shape and redefine the world through their imaginative thinking, pushing the boundaries of what is possible and inspiring others to do the same.

The ability to generate innovative ideas, solutions, and approaches becomes a crucial asset in navigating complexities, fostering progress, and adapting to change.

Creative Thinking as a Fundamental Skill:

Creative thinking is not confined to specific industries or professions. It has become a fundamental skill applicable across diverse fields.

The capacity to approach problems with an open mind, think critically, and generate original ideas is essential in addressing the multifaceted challenges of the modern world.

Creative Economy

The creative economy emphasizes the economic significance of creativity, culture, and intellectual property. It includes activities that are based on individual creativity, skill, and talent with the potential for wealth and job creation through the generation and exploitation of intellectual property.

Creative Industries

Creative industries encompass vital sectors such as arts and culture, design, media, and entertainment. These dynamic fields not only contribute significantly to cultural enrichment but also play a pivotal role in driving economic growth. The arts foster creativity and self-expression, design shapes the aesthetic fabric of products and environments, media disseminates information and influences public opinion, and entertainment captivates and delights audiences worldwide. Together, these sectors form the vibrant tapestry of creative industries, influencing societal trends, stimulating innovation, and contributing substantially to the cultural and economic fabric of nations.

Protecting creations(Intellectual Property- IPR)

Intellectual property refers to intangible creations of the mind, and its protection and exploitation are crucial considerations in various fields. This encompasses elements such as patents, copyrights, trademarks, and other forms of legal safeguards. Patents protect inventions, copyrights guard original works of authorship, and trademarks secure distinctive symbols identifying products or services. The legal framework surrounding intellectual property

not only safeguards the rights of creators and inventors but also incentivizes innovation and creativity by ensuring that individuals and organizations can benefit from their intellectual endeavors. The strategic exploitation of intellectual property involves maximizing its value through licensing, collaborations, or commercialization, contributing to economic growth and fostering a culture of innovation.

6

Prioritizing User Needs and Experiences

Human-centric development prioritizes human needs, experiences, and values in creating products and services, emphasizing the user's perspective, preferences, behaviors, and well-being. In the realm of hyper-personalization, this approach extends to understanding individual characteristics, influencing not just user interfaces but also underlying processes, policies, and technologies. In enterprise development, embracing a human-centric approach signals a commitment to empathy, inclusivity, and ongoing improvement. By centering on genuine user needs, this approach enhances satisfaction, contributing positively to the overall human experience within the enterprise ecosystem.

This term emphasizes the importance of putting human needs, experiences, and values at the forefront of the development process. It aligns with the idea of designing products and services that prioritize the user's perspective, considering their preferences, behaviors, and overall well-being.

In the context of hyper-personalization, a human-centric approach implies that technology and business solutions are developed with a deep understanding of individuals and their unique characteristics. It encompasses not only the user interface and experience but also the underlying processes, policies, and technologies that support personalized interactions.

By adopting a human-centric approach in enterprise development, organizations acknowledge the significance of empathy, inclusivity, and continuous improvement. It reflects a commitment to creating solutions that genuinely address user needs, enhance user satisfaction, and contribute positively to the overall human experience within the enterprise ecosystem.Designing customer-centric products in the era of hyper-personalization requires a deep understanding of individual customer needs, preferences, and behaviors. Here are key principles and strategies for creating products that prioritize the customer experience in a hyper-personalized environment:

Customer Understanding

•	Data-driven Insights: Leverage advanced analytics and machine learning to gather and analyze customer data. Understand their preferences, behaviors, and journey across various touchpoints.
•	User Research: Conduct extensive user research to gain qualitative insights into customer motivations, pain points, and desires.

Personalized User Interface (UI) and User Experience (UX)

•	Dynamic Content: Create interfaces that can adapt based on user preferences and behavior. Tailor content, layout, and features to individual users.
•	Intuitive Design: Ensure the product's design is intuitive and easy to navigate, with personalized elements seamlessly integrated into the overall user experience.
Context-aware Features

•	Contextual Recommendations: Provide real-time, context-aware recommendations based on user interactions, location, or current activities.
•	Adaptive Features: Build features that adapt to users' changing needs and preferences over time.

Permission-based Personalization:

•	Transparent Opt-in: Clearly communicate the value of personalization and seek user consent. Allow users to control the level of personalization and the data they are comfortable sharing.
•	Privacy by Design: Implement robust privacy measures to protect customer data and build trust.

AI and Machine Learning Integration

•	Predictive Algorithms: Utilize predictive algorithms to anticipate user needs and proactively offer solutions.
•	Continuous Learning: Implement systems that continuously learn from user interactions and feedback, refining personalization over time.
Omnichannel Consistency

•	Seamless Cross-platform Experience: Ensure a consistent and personalized experience across various channels, such as web, mobile, social media, and physical stores.

•	Unified Customer Profiles: Create a unified customer profile that consolidates data from different touchpoints for a holistic understanding.
Feedback Mechanisms

•	Continuous Feedback Loop: Establish mechanisms for gathering customer feedback on personalization efforts. Use this feedback to iterate and improve the personalized experience.

•	Responsive to Changes: Be agile in adapting to changing customer preferences and market trends.

Agile Development and Iteration

•	Rapid Prototyping: Embrace agile development methodologies and rapid prototyping to quickly test and iterate on personalized features.

•	Iterative Improvement: Continuously iterate on the product based on user feedback and emerging trends.
Human-Centered Approach

•	Empathy in Design: Prioritize empathy in the design process, understanding the emotional aspects of user interactions.

•	Inclusive Design: Ensure that personalization efforts are inclusive and consider diverse user needs and preferences.
Measuring Success

•	Key Performance Indicators (KPIs): Define and track KPIs that reflect the success of personalization efforts, such as user engagement, satisfaction, and conversion rates.

• A/B Testing: A/B testing is a method of comparing two versions of a personalization strategy to determine which performs better. The term "A/B" signifies the comparison between two variants: "A" and "B." By randomly segmenting users and measuring key metrics, it identifies the most effective approach to enhance user engagement, conversions, or other defined goals. A/B testing is an effective way to determine the best personalization strategies for engaging users. Use A/B testing to experiment with different personalization strategies and identify what resonates best with users.

In summary, designing customer-centric products in the era of hyper-personalization involves leveraging advanced technologies, understanding individual customer needs, and continuously adapting based on user feedback and emerging trends. The key is to create a seamless, intuitive, and empathetic experience that adds value to each customer's unique journey.

7

Design Thinking in Entrepreneurship

The integration of design thinking into entrepreneurship represents a paradigm shift, propelling businesses towards customer-centric innovation and sustainable growth. By understanding and addressing the needs of end-users, entrepreneurs employing design thinking not only stay ahead of the curve but also contribute to creating a future where their ventures thrive and make a meaningful impact.

In the fast-paced and ever-evolving landscape of entrepreneurship, the keys to success often lie in understanding user needs, solving complex problems, and fostering innovation.

The design thinking approach, a systematic and intuitive methodology with a strong focus on customer outcomes, has emerged as a powerful tool for entrepreneurs navigating the dynamic business environment. This chapter explores the keys of enterprise design thinking and its transformative impact on entrepreneurial endeavors.

The Keys of Enterprise Design Thinking

Enterprise Design Thinking places a significant emphasis on user outcomes and problem-solving through diverse teams. By understanding the users' needs and aspirations, the approach aligns entrepreneurial efforts with creating solutions that genuinely matter.

The Evolution of Design Thinking in Entrepreneurship

Design thinking is more than a methodology; it is a way of using systemic reasoning and intuition to explore ideal future states. Traditionally, design focused on aesthetics, but in the entrepreneurial landscape, it has evolved into a dynamic concept that shapes problem-solving approaches in response to rapidly changing environments. This evolution positions design as both a journey and a destination, with design thinking serving as a core methodology to initiate and guide the journey, ensuring organizations reach the right destination at the right time.

Customer-Centric Problem Solving

At its core, design thinking means fundamentally changing how products, services, and organizations are developed. It entails putting customers, employees, and the planet at the center of problem-solving. In the entrepreneurial context, this shift is crucial as it aligns business strategies with the genuine needs of the market. Design thinking is not just a process; it's a philosophy that resonates with the ethos of entrepreneurial ventures aiming to create lasting impact and shareholder value.

*The Design Thinking Process in
Entrepreneurship*

The design thinking process begins by delving into the needs, dreams, and behaviors of end-users. Teams practice empathetic listening to discern what users truly want, steering clear of preconceived notions. The focus then shifts to devising solutions that authentically address these needs from the user's perspective.

Unveiling Future Needs through Understanding

Beyond the current needs, design thinking in entrepreneurship involves developing an understanding of behavior and needs that transcends the present, anticipating what users will require in the future. Spending time with people becomes integral to this process, allowing entrepreneurs to gain insights that go beyond immediate concerns and envision solutions that stand the test of time.

Iterative Concepting and Rapid Prototyping

"Concepting," iterating, and testing are pivotal phases in the design thinking process. Entrepreneurs sketch out concepts on paper and swiftly translate them into rough prototypes. The emphasis on speed in this phase allows for rapid feedback loops, enabling refinement and continuous testing. This iterative approach is fundamental to the entrepreneurial spirit, where agility and adaptability are key to success. The integration of design thinking into entrepreneurship represents a paradigm shift, propelling businesses towards customer-centric innovation and sustainable growth. By understanding and addressing the needs of end-users, entrepreneurs employing design thinking not only stay ahead of the curve but also contribute to creating a future where their ventures thrive and make a meaningful impact.

TOWARDS BUILDING YOUR BUSINESS

STARTING THE JOURNEY

KEY QUESTIONS:
- GOAL OF YOUR BUSINESS/OR YOUR ENTREPRENEURIAL VENTURE:
- IDENTIFYING USER NEEDS
- USER OR CUSTOMER CENTRIC BUSINESS
- IDENTIFYING WHAT SERVICES OR PRODUCTS THAT THE USERS NEE

Crafting Your Enterprise Research Plan
GOAL: To understand customer/user needs market, challenges, main questions to address through services or products, users, their problems

<table>
<tr><td>OPEN YOUR EYES</td><td>OPEN YOUR MIND</td><td>OPEN YOUR HEART</td></tr>
<tr><td>Go out and start learning</td><td colspan="2">Travel, observe, interact with diverse culture</td></tr>
</table>

The initial stride in constructing your project involves conceiving an idea, a concept that possesses a demand.

Follow the process (This is part of designing and developing your enterprise and start of your entrepreneurial journey)

Open Your Eyes
Entrepreneurial research necessitates observation. Open your eyes to unveil hidden insights and user perspectives. Being observant and attuned to the world around you is pivotal for entrepreneurship in today's context.

Seek concealed insights and user perspectives to comprehend the needs of your target market and formulate innovative products and services.

Economies that have achieved advanced status have gleaned knowledge from others.

Historically, students from advanced nations embarked on journeys to understand diverse cultures and lifestyles.

Leading projects in today's global economy are products of extensive research, learning from behavioural patterns, and understanding diverse global communities/cultures encompassing their needs, preferences, and cultures.

Expand your horizons

Embracing differences is pivotal; an open mindset is indispensable.

Open-minded entrepreneurs are more prone to generating innovative ideas and establishing successful businesses. They demonstrate adaptability to change and resilience in overcoming challenges.

Ways to foster an open mind include:

Be willing to learn from others.

• Engage with fellow entrepreneurs.
• Read books and articles about entrepreneurship.
• Attend conferences and workshops to expand knowledge.
• Challenge assumptions and explore alternative approaches.
• Embrace experimentation and take calculated risks.
• Welcome feedback, even when critical, as it aids improvement.

Open Your Heart

In the research process of designing your enterprise project, immerse yourself in learning from other users and communities.

Place yourself in another person's shoes and genuinely

understand or share their experiences within their unique perspective and context.

Tips for this phase include:

• Document your observations.
• Cultivate a mindset conducive to creativity and original thinking.
• Identify real-world challenges and conceptualize ideas to address them.
• Approach the journey with a problem-solving mindset, aiming to enhance the human experience

Design Research Plan

Compile a list of all ideas, product concepts, or other notions that have surfaced in your mind.

SHORTLIST AND FINALISE A CONCEPT:

CONCEPT/IDEA

DESCRIBE(GIVE DETAILED DESCRIPTION
VALUE PROPOSITION

TARGET CUSTOMERS/USERS

WHO ARE NOT YOUR TARGET COMMUNITIES OR USERS

BENEFITS

What is the VISION behind your business?

Which problem are you going to solve?

What do you want to achieve?

WHAT IS THE VISION BEHIND YOUR BUSINESS?
BUSINESS MAD LIB word game*

To create a Business Madlib, simply replace the blanks in a Mad Lib template with business-related words and phrases.

------------------------------------- CONCEPT NAME-

IS A ---------------------(provide description

------------------------for (customers/TARGET USERS)

--(That (€) ----------------------

(value proposition) ----------------------------------

enabling (benefits) -----------------------------------

***Business Madlib is a term used to describe the use of Mad Libs, a popular word game, to create business-related content.**

WHAT DO YOU NEED TO LEARN?

• *List everything you need to learn in order to know, if your idea will be a success.*
• *What are the uncertainties you have?*
• *List the major questions you want to answer about people you are designing or developing*
your business or questions you want to explore.
Who are the people or groups you want to learn from?
Who Are Your Learning Resources?

CUSTOMERS and END USERS

• *These should be your best guess at who your customer or the end user could be.*
• *Identify who you want to meet and why?*
• *List out questions to be asked to them?*
• *What is the objective of an interaction or data collection from them?*
• *Or why and what kind of information to be gathered and from whom?*
In addition to your users or customers:
Also, identify:

OTHER PARTNERS or those who must involve in your research to collect valuable insights:
This may be:

• *A person or few who are not directly related to your industry but who can offer*
important perspective

Identify:
*OTHER PARTNERS or those who must involve in
your research to collect valuable insights:*
This may be:
*• A person or few who are not directly related to your
industry but who can offer
important perspectives*

*• KEY STAKEHOLDERS who you should under-
stand and learn from*
*• Persons: who influence purchase decision or of people
who matters in influencing a decision maker or a user/
customer*
*• Anyone from a different industry but with significant
experience who can give you a new way of thinking or
perspective*
*• Any other person from whom you can learn ? It could
be upto you based on your interactions and discussions*

*RESEARCH METHOD AND GATHERING
KEY INPUTS FOR YOUR BUSINESS*

User interviews:
*One-on-one interviews with potential users to understand
their needs, wants, and pain points.*

Focus groups
*Group discussions with potential users to get feedback on
ideas and concepts.*

Ethnographic research
Observing potential users in their natural environment to understand their behavior and needs.

Brainstorming
A group activity to generate a large number of ideas, without judgment

THE ENTERPRISE DESGING RESEARCH PLAN

MATCH A QUESTION OR A CONCEPT/CHALLENGE WITH A CORE USER OR CUSTOMERS AND A METHOD

- Collecting data for answering specific questions or for business idea/concept
- (For each question select appropriate research method, objective and target customers)

MAIN THEME or Question

Who do you want to learn this from?

How will you reach this target group of users or probable customers?

Research Method

8

Multicultural Entrepreneurship

Multicultural entrepreneurship harnesses diverse backgrounds to fuel innovation and build successful businesses, going beyond business solely to integrate cultural strengths for a competitive edge.

In today's interconnected and globalized world, the buzzwords of diversity and multiculturalism have transformed into powerful catalysts for change within modern societies. The dynamic interplay of cultures, perspectives, and experiences has become integral to the realms of entrepreneurship, creativity, and innovation. This chapter explores the profound implications of multiculturalism and diversity in the business landscape, shedding light on the benefits and impact these concepts have on the world of entrepreneurship.

The Foundation of Multiculturalism

The Oxford Dictionary provides a comprehensive definition of multiculturalism, emphasizing its inclusivity across various races, religions, languages, and traditions. Diversity, as defined by Kelli A. Green, goes beyond mere acknowledgment; it involves understanding, accepting, valuing, and celebrating differences across a spectrum of attributes, from age and gender to ethnicity and ability. In the business context, managing a multicultural workforce extends beyond mere representation to changing mindsets and organizational culture, aligning with broader strategic goals.

Cultivating Cultural Literacy in Leadership

In the global economy, cultural literacy emerges as a key competence for business leaders. Rosen and Digh argue that successful leaders should be "inquisitive internationalists," respecting their own cultural heritage while looking beyond it for opportunities. The concept of a "respectful modernizer" encourages retaining the best of one's culture while leveraging the knowledge of others. A "culture bridger" forms alliances across cultures, and a "global capitalist" brings global resources to local challenges and vice versa. In essence, cultural literacy becomes an essential skill for navigating multicultural situations, teams, and markets.

Multicultural Workforce

Multicultural enterprises reap numerous benefits. Companies that prioritize diversity tend to be more profitable and successful, as they can tap into a wealth of ideas and perspectives. Cross-cultural teamwork and collaboration become essential for productivity, with diversity viewed not as a liability but as an asset. The advantages of a multicultural workforce extend to marketing opportunities, enhanced creativity and innovation, improved business image, and a competitive edge.

Maximizing the Potential: Benefits of Multicultural Enterprises

The advantages of multicultural enterprises are manifold. Creating a bond between employer and employee, exponentially increasing marketing opportunities, stimulating creativity and innovation, enhancing business image, attracting diverse talent, and gaining a competitive edge are just a few. In a workplace that values diversity, interpersonal and personal aspects flourish, contributing to higher turnout and increased productivity.

Entrepreneurship

Diversity also has a profound impact on entrepreneurship. Diverse teams bring enhanced innovation, market expansion, risk-taking, and resilience. A diverse and inclusive workplace attracts top talent, contributing to a dynamic and skilled workforce. Entrepreneurs, when exposed to multicultural environments, gain a broader perspective, identifying unmet needs and opportunities in the global market.

Creativity and Multiculturalism & Diversity

Multicultural environments serve as breeding grounds for creativity and innovation. Cross-cultural collaboration sparks creative ideas, cultural fusion leads to unique products and expressions, and exposure to different cultures promotes open-mindedness. Global perspectives gained through multicultural experiences empower entrepreneurs to think creatively and adapt to an ever-changing market landscape.

Diversity and multiculturalism are not mere trends but powerful drivers of positive change in entrepreneurship, creativity, and innovation. Embracing diversity unlocks a broader range of talents and experiences, leading to innovative solutions and a more inclusive society. By fostering diversity, entrepreneurs and innovators harness the collective power of different cultures to drive positive change, creating a brighter and more prosperous future for all.

9

Economic Reforms
Paving the Way for New Opportunities

The economic reforms of 1991 in India heralded a new era of opportunity for the Indian youth. These reforms, characterized by liberalization, privatization, and globalization, brought about significant positive changes. Entrepreneurial opportunities flourished, as the reforms simplified business establishment and management, providing a platform for innovative young minds to explore their ideas.

With the opening up of various sectors and the expansion of industries, job creation soared, offering a plethora of employment options to the young workforce. Simultaneously, entrepreneurship flourished, as the reforms simplified business establishment and management, providing a platform for innovative young minds to explore their ideas.

The surge in economic activity also bolstered the demand for higher education and vocational training, equipping the youth with the skills needed for better job prospects. Moreover, the global exposure resulting from globalization empowered Indian youth to compete on a global scale, fostering a spirit of innovation and competitiveness.

With economic growth came increased incomes, enabling young people to enhance their living standards and save for the future. Rapid urbanization, driven by economic growth, led to the creation of urban centers with better infrastructure, drawing youth seeking improved living conditions and job opportunities.

The reforms expanded the financial sector, promoting greater financial inclusion and providing the youth with better access to banking and financial services, thereby broadening their economic horizons.

The complexities of brand establishment and marketing, once formidable and cost-intensive, have now become significantly more accessible.

In contemporary times, initiating a business venture has become markedly more straightforward, with a streamlined process that experts and international agencies and our own experience prove that its 80% faster. An array of digital tools and infrastructure is available virtually cost-free.

Furthermore, India's expansive market offers a multitude of opportunities for entrepreneurs and small and medium-sized enterprises (SMEs). From agriculturists and artisans to cottage industries and SMEs, the business arena and marketplace beckon for exploration and expansion.

These monumental changes transcend mere reforms; they signify a revolution reshaping the narrative of India's business landscape. The new India is of opportunities. It's the coming back and revival in full strength India's entrepreneurial legacy.

The New Economic Policy of 1991

In the early 1990s, India confronted a significant economic crisis marked by a foreign exchange deficit, precipitating a pronounced economic downturn. In response to this predicament, the government initiated a series of economic adjustments through a package of reforms known as 'structural reforms' under the rubric of the 'New Economic Policy (NEP).

The New Economic Policy encompass a suite of economic-policy initiatives and various policy instruments aimed at bolstering macroeconomic stability.

These measures include stabilization actions designed to curb inflation and rectify the Balance of Payments (BoP) crisis, as well as structural reform measures intended to enhance economic efficiency and heighten international competitiveness.

The objectives of the New Economic Policy, 1991, were multifaceted

- To integrate the Indian economy into the global arena, charting a new course for the Indian market.
- To mitigate inflation rates and accumulate foreign exchange reserves, thereby accelerating economic growth.
- To increase private sector participation in economic growth by reducing government-controlled sectors.
- To facilitate the global flow of goods, services, capital, human resources, and technology by reducing trade constraints.

- To attain economic stability and create an unencumbered economic market by eliminating superfluous trade and tariff restrictions.

Structural Reforms: Liberalization, Privatization, and Globalization

The components of the New Economic Policy, 1991, revolved around three pivotal concepts: Liberalization, Privatization, and Globalization.

This model supplanted the earlier Licence Raj. The prime goal of these reforms was to stimulate rapid economic growth, lower inflation rates, reduce fiscal deficits, and rectify the BoP crisis.

Liberalization

Liberalization is a cornerstone of the NEP, signaling a shift from government control to a more open and market-driven economic system.

Prior to 1991, the government held sway over the private sector, hampering decision-making within domestic industries. The liberalization policy sought to empower these sectors with greater autonomy, eliminating government interference.

The government's abolition of the licensing system was instrumental in streamlining industrial activities, reducing bureaucratic delays and corruption. Under the Liberalization Policy, various economic reforms were introduced, including those in the industrial sector, financial sector, tax regime, foreign exchange, and trade and investment policies.

Privatization

Privatization involves the transfer of ownership and operation of public sector enterprises to the private sector. This transition was necessitated by the underperformance of public sector undertakings, which resulted in poor product quality and services for consumers. Privatization promotes diversification, higher profits, customer satisfaction, productivity, and growth, all within a competitive environment.

Integration with the global economy

Globalization is the integration of the Indian economy with the global arena, fostering the free flow of trade, capital, information, technology, and people. This process enhances economic development by facilitating collaboration with multinational corporations, reducing trade barriers, promoting exports, and attracting investments and promoting collaborations..

The reform measures included opening the market to foreign investments and international trade, reducing reliance on foreign loans, expanding the banking and capital sectors, increasing competition through privatization, and improving the quality of goods and services.

Globalization contributed in connecting the local market with the global economy. It significantly enhanced exposure for local markets & stakeholders to the enterprises, collaboration opoortunities from across the world. Indeed it also reduced international trade restrictions, with opportunties for local comapnies access overseas markets. Ultimately it enhances India's position in the global markets.

KEY REFORMS ENHANCING EASE OF DOING BUSINESS IN INDIA

Here are some key areas where reforms have been implemented to foster ease of doing business in India:

1. Simplified Business Registration:
India has streamlined the process of starting a business by introducing online registration platforms.

Entrepreneurs can now register their businesses more easily and quickly, reducing bureaucratic hurdles.

2. Single Window Clearance:
The introduction of single window clearance systems streamlines the process of obtaining various licenses and permits.

This centralized platform allows businesses to submit applications and receive clearances from multiple government departments, saving time and reducing administrative burden.

3. Tax Reforms:

The Goods and Services Tax (GST) has replaced multiple indirect taxes, unifying the tax structure across the country.

This has simplified the tax compliance process for businesses and reduced the complexity of doing business in different states.

4. Insolvency and Bankruptcy Code (IBC):
The IBC has strengthened the legal framework for resolving insolvency cases.

It provides a more efficient and time-bound process for debt recovery, increasing investor confidence and improving the ease of exiting businesses.

5. Labour Reforms:

Labour laws have been rationalized to provide flexibility to businesses while protecting workers' rights.

The introduction of labor codes has simplified and consolidated various labor laws, promoting ease of compliance for businesses.

6. Digital Initiatives:
India has embraced digitalization in various sectors, including business registration, tax filings, and compliance procedures.

Online platforms and digital services have made it easier for businesses to interact with government departments and complete necessary procedures remotely.

7. Infrastructure Development:

Focusing on improvement in physical infrastructure, such as roads, ports, and logistics networks. Enhances connectivity, reduces transportation costs, and facilitates the movement of goods and services across the country.

8. Investor Protection:

Measures have been taken to strengthen investor protection and corporate governance norms. This includes greater transparency, disclosure requirements, and enhanced mechanisms for resolving shareholder disputes.

These ease of doing business reforms in India have resulted in significant improvements in the World Bank's Doing Business rankings. They have helped attract investments, foster entrepreneurship, and create a more conducive environment for businesses to thrive. The government continues to prioritize reforms to further enhance the ease of doing business in the country, promoting economic growth and development.

Reduction in Compliance Burden:

GOI (Central Ministries, states, and UTs) have decriminalized more than 3,500 provisions related to minor technical or procedural defaults (Source: Economic Survey 2022-23).
Reduced more than 39,000 compliances to foster ease of doing business as of January 17, 2023, according to the Economic Survey 2022-23.
New technologies will further reduce the compliance burden, including monitoring of transactions, payments, labor-related aspects, and supply chain monitoring.
India has emerged as one of the most attractive destinations not only for investments but also for doing business.

10

Framework to Understand Emerging Business Opportunities: Key Aspect to Focus

Entrepreneurs can unlock immense business opportunities by aligning their ventures with sustainability principles, SDGs, and global trends. This alignment can be achieved through responsible practices, digital initiatives, and stakeholder collaboration. Key sectors like renewable energy, agriculture, tourism, and waste management offer significant potential for youth entrepreneurs to drive economic growth, empower communities, and promote green practices.

It is crucial for entrepreneurs to align their enterprise goals, operations, products, and services with the principles of sustainability, Sustainable development goals(SDGs) and key global market trends and economic policies. This alignment can be achieved by integrating these aspects into their business strategies, adopting responsible practices, promoting innovation, and collaborating with stakeholders to address specific sustainable development challenges in alignment with the policy framework. By doing so, these industries and SMEs can work in harmony with larger global market trends and preferences.

The Sustainable Development Goals (SDGs) provide a comprehensive framework for future economic activities and models to focus on. SDGs encompass a wide range of social, economic, and environmental objectives.

Renewable Energy Industry

The renewable energy industry plays a crucial role in achieving SDG 7 (Affordable and Clean Energy). By investing in and promoting renewable energy sources such as solar, wind, and hydroelectric power, this industry contributes to reducing greenhouse gas emissions, improving energy access, and promoting sustainable energy practices.

Sustainable Agriculture and Food Industry: SDG 2 (Zero Hunger) and SDG 12 (Responsible Consumption and Production) are closely linked to the agriculture and food industry.

SMEs in this sector can promote sustainable farming practices, reduce food waste, and support local and organic food production. Adopting sustainable supply chains and promoting fair trade can also contribute to SDG 8 (Decent Work and Economic Growth).

Responsible Tourism and Hospitality Industry

The tourism and hospitality industry have a significant impact on several SDGs, including SDG 8 (Decent Work and Economic Growth), SDG 11 (Sustainable Cities and Communities), and SDG 12 (Responsible Consumption and Production). SMEs in this sector can adopt sustainable practices, promote cultural preservation, support local communities, and minimize environmental impacts through responsible tourism initiatives.

Circular Economy and Waste Management

Industry: SDG 12 (Responsible Consumption and Production) is directly related to the circular economy and waste management industry. SMEs can focus on reducing waste generation, recycling and reusing materials, and promoting sustainable consumption patterns. This industry contributes to resource efficiency, waste reduction, and mitigating environmental pollution.

Education and Skill Development Industry

SDG 4 (Quality Education) and SDG 8 (Decent Work and Economic Growth) are central to the education and skill development industry. SMEs in this sector can provide vocational training, promote lifelong learning opportunities, and support inclusive education. By equipping individuals with skills for sustainable employment, they contribute to poverty reduction and economic empowerment.

Key sectors and markets

Opportunities for Youth Entrepreneurs

There are immense business opportunities for youth entrepreneurs to contribute to and support the agriculture-farm economy, small and micro enterprises, and rural economy through:

Digital Marketing

o   Huge market potential: 80% of e-commerce is currently B2B, leaving a vast untapped B2C segment (20%).

o	Local, regional, and national e-commerce platforms: Capitalize on the rapidly growing global e-commerce market (US$16.6 trillion in 2022) and tailor platforms to connect rural producers with consumers.

o	Example: India's online retail market is expected to reach US$325 billion by 2030, offering significant opportunities for rural product sales.

•	Digital Marketing for Agriculture and Rural Products:

o	Leverage digital marketing: Utilize online content, social media, and targeted campaigns to connect farmers and rural entrepreneurs with wider audiences (domestic and international).

•	Digital Transformation in Agriculture and Rural Businesses:

o	Drive efficiency, productivity, and innovation: Develop solutions like farm management software, IoT-enabled devices, and supply chain optimization platforms.

•	Export Promotion for Rural Products:

o	Connect rural producers with global buyers: Facilitate export networks, provide market intelligence, and assist with certifications and compliance.

•	eCommerce Facilitation for Rural Entrepreneurs:

o	Empower online presence: Assist with website development, online store setup, logistics, and payment gateways.

o   Example: Help rural entrepreneurs overcome geographical limitations and reach a wider customer base through e-commerce platforms.

By pursuing these avenues, youth entrepreneurs can drive economic growth, empower rural communities, and promote sustainability in these crucial sectors. Their unique skills and perspectives are vital for harnessing the transformative power of digital technologies for the benefit of agricultural and rural economies.

11

Unlocking Opportunities in the Farm Sector and Agro-based Enterprises

Through innovative solutions, market linkages, financial inclusion, and capacity building, entrepreneurs can play a transformative role in empowering farmers, improving agricultural productivity, and realizing the ambitious goal of doubling farmer incomes.

The Agenda of Doubling Farmer Income (DFI) is not just a policy initiative; it is a transformative vision that presents a significant opportunity for entrepreneurs to play a pivotal role in supporting farmer communities and organizations. This chapter explores the various facets of this agenda and outlines key areas where entrepreneurs can make a substantial impact.

1. Dairy Cooperatives: A Foundation for Growth

In India, the dairy sector stands as a cornerstone of agricultural livelihoods. With close to 30 dairy Milk Cooperative Federations and approximately two lakh primary dairy societies, the foundation for dairy-based entrepreneurship is already laid. Plans to expand these cooperatives, with each village housing a primary agriculture society, provide entrepreneurs with a massive canvas to contribute to the DFI agenda.

2. FPOs/FPCs: Catalyzing Agricultural Transformation

Farmers Producer Organizations (FPOs) and Farmers Producer Companies (FPCs) are on the rise, numbering close to 18,000 by 2023 and steadily growing. These entities are becoming key players in reshaping the agricultural landscape. Entrepreneurs can actively engage with and support FPOs and FPCs, acting as catalysts for agricultural transformation and income enhancement.

3. Agricultural Technology and Services: Innovating for Productivity

Entrepreneurs can drive the DFI agenda by developing and providing innovative agricultural technologies, tools, and services. Precision farming solutions, farm management software, modern machinery, and efficient irrigation systems all contribute to improving productivity and reducing costs for farmers. By offering these solutions, entrepreneurs become integral partners in achieving the goal of doubling farmer incomes.

4. Value Chain Enhancement: Adding Value, Increasing Incomes

Strengthening the agricultural value chain is paramount to the DFI agenda. Entrepreneurs can focus on establishing efficient post-harvest management systems, storage facilities, processing units, and value-added product development. By reducing post-harvest losses and adding value to agricultural produce, entrepreneurs contribute to farmers fetching better prices and, in turn, increasing their incomes.

5. Market Linkages and Access: Bridging Gaps for Farmers

Facilitating direct market linkages is a critical avenue for entrepreneurs. By establishing connections between farmers and consumers, retailers, and exporters, entrepreneurs can set up cooperatives, online platforms, and distribution networks. These initiatives ensure fair prices, reduce middlemen, and provide farmers with access to wider markets, directly impacting their income potential.

6. Financial Inclusion and Access to Credit: Empowering Farmers

Entrepreneurs can facilitate financial inclusion by offering microfinance, crop insurance, and credit solutions tailored for farmers. Timely and affordable credit empowers farmers to invest in modern farming practices, purchase high-quality inputs, and enhance overall productivity and profitability.

7. Capacity Building and Skill Development: Nurturing Innovation in Farming

Contributing to doubling farmer incomes goes beyond tangible solutions; it involves empowering farmers with knowledge and skills. Entrepreneurs can initiate training, capacity building, and skill development programs focused on sustainable farming practices, advanced agricultural techniques, market intelligence, and entrepreneurship skills. By doing so, they foster a culture of innovation and entrepreneurship within the farming community.

In conclusion, the Agenda of Doubling Farmer Income presents a vast array of opportunities for entrepreneurs to actively contribute to the prosperity of farmer communities and organizations. Through innovative solutions, market linkages, financial inclusion, and capacity building, entrepreneurs can play a transformative role in empowering farmers, improving agricultural productivity, and realizing the ambitious goal of doubling farmer incomes.

HUM Shilpakar - Digital Marketplace for Artisan Entrepreneurs

In response to the imperative need for bestowing a digital identity and market access upon the Indian artisan community, the initiative known as "HUM SHILPAKAR" was established. HUM SHILPAKAR is a social media-based platform meticulously designed to assist artisans in connecting with potential buyers and discovering markets for their exceptional products.

The Indian handloom and handicraft sector, celebrated for its labor-intensive production methods, encompasses an array of high-value products, including Indian silk dresses, pottery, and handmade items crafted by skilled artists and artisans. Regret-

tably, manufacturers of these products have encountered challenges over time, resulting in the disappearance of their distinctive creations.

Recognizing the imperative to preserve and promote these environmentally friendly and culturally rich products, the HUM Shilpakar network, also known as the Artisans Network, conducted an in-depth study. The study revealed a concerning decline in the number of manufacturers and the gradual disappearance of thousands of unique Indian products from the market.

To address this pressing issue, the HUM Shilpakar network has taken the proactive initiative to provide a digital identity for manufacturers, cottage-based activities, potters, weavers, and handicraftsmen. Through the creation of a dedicated platform, artisans can showcase their products, connect with potential buyers, and access broader markets beyond their villages or panchayats.

The HUM Shilpakar platform serves as a vital bridge between artisans and buyers, facilitating the discovery and engagement with a diverse range of Indian handicrafts and handmade products. Leveraging social media tools and features, artisans can share their stories, showcase their unique skills, and capture the attention of buyers who appreciate the beauty and craftsmanship of these products.

By harnessing the power of technology and social media platforms, the HUM Shilpakar network aims to revitalize the market presence of Indian artisans and their distinctive creations. This initiative not only promotes economic empowerment for artisans but also fosters the preservation of traditional craftsmanship, cultural heritage, and environmentally friendly practices.

The HUM SHILPAKAR initiative, orchestrated by the Artisans Network, is dedicated to providing a digital identity and market access for Indian artisans. Through a social media-based platform, this initiative endeavors to revive disappearing manufacturers and their unique, environmentally friendly products, contributing to economic empowerment and the preservation of India's rich artisanal heritage.

12

Fourth Industrial Revolution

Digital economy, Gig workers, Sharing economy, platforms, Industry 4.0

Digital Economy: This refers to economic activity facilitated by digital technologies, encompassing e-commerce, online banking, social media, and more. It's reshaping entire industries and creating new avenues for businesses and individuals.

Gig Workers: These are individuals who don't have traditional full-time jobs but instead earn income through short-term tasks or projects obtained through online platforms. Think Uber drivers, freelance writers, or delivery personnel. The gig economy offers flexibility and independence but also raises concerns about job security and worker benefits.

Sharing Economy: This model involves accessing resources or services through temporary ownership or peer-to-peer interaction, facilitated by platforms like Airbnb, car-sharing services, or tool libraries. It promotes efficient resource utilization and sustainability while creating new income streams for individuals.

Platforms: These are the digital marketplaces that connect gig workers, consumers, and service providers in the digital economy and sharing economy. They play a crucial role in matching supply and demand, facilitating transactions, and managing data.

Industry 4.0: This term refers to the fourth industrial revolution, driven by technologies like automation, artificial intelligence, robotics, and the Internet of Things (IoT). It's transforming manufacturing, logistics, and various other sectors, bringing increased efficiency, productivity, and customization.

The digital economy and platforms provide the infrastructure for gig and sharing economies to thrive. Meanwhile, Industry 4.0 technologies are further automating and optimizing processes within these models. Overall, this interconnected web of concepts is shaping the future of work, consumption, and resource utilization.

The Fourth Industrial Revolution, marked by the convergence of digital, physical, and biological technologies, presents a dynamic landscape for small and medium-sized enterprises (SMEs). To not only survive but thrive in this transformative era, SMEs must proactively address challenges and seize opportunities through comprehensive strategies.

1. Digital Transformation: Paving the Way for Competitiveness

Embracing digital transformation is not just an option; it is a necessity for SMEs aiming to remain competitive in the Fourth Industrial Revolution. This involves adopting cutting-edge technologies like cloud computing, data analytics, artificial intelligence, and the Internet of Things (IoT). By integrating these tools, SMEs can streamline operations, improve efficiency, and elevate customer experiences. Furthermore, a strategic shift towards e-commerce and online platforms can significantly expand the reach of SMEs, connecting them to new markets and a broader customer base.

2. Innovation and Agility: Cultivating a Culture of Progress

In the Fourth Industrial Revolution, innovation and agility are not just buzzwords but guiding principles for success. SMEs should foster a culture of innovation within their organizations, encouraging employees to think creatively and adapt swiftly to technological advancements. By embracing new ideas, experimenting with emerging technologies, and maintaining a mindset open to change, SMEs can position themselves ahead of the curve and capitalize on emerging business opportunities.

3. Collaboration and Networking: The Power of Connectivity

Surviving and thriving in the Fourth Industrial Revolution requires SMEs to embrace collaboration and networking. Joining industry networks, participating in innovation ecosystems, and establishing collaborations with larger companies, research institutions, and startups can unlock access to crucial resources, knowledge, and partnerships. These collaborative efforts enhance competitiveness, spur growth, and create a synergistic environment for innovation.

4. Talent Development and Upskilling: Nurturing a Skilled Workforce

To meet the demands of the Fourth Industrial Revolution, SMEs must invest in talent development and upskilling programs. Ensuring that the workforce is proficient in emerging technologies is paramount. SMEs can achieve this through comprehensive training initiatives, forging partnerships with educational institutions, and active participation in government-led skill development programs. A skilled workforce is the backbone of innovation and adaptability.

5. Cybersecurity and Data Privacy: Safeguarding Digital Assets

As SMEs traverse the digital landscape, prioritizing cybersecurity and data privacy is non-negotiable. Robust cybersecurity measures must be implemented to safeguard sensitive business and customer data. Additionally, understanding and complying with relevant data privacy regulations are crucial not only for legal adherence but also to maintain trust with customers and business partners.

6. Access to Finance and Funding: Overcoming Financial Hurdles

Access to finance remains a significant challenge for SMEs venturing into technological investments and innovation. Governments and financial institutions play a pivotal role in supporting SMEs in the Fourth Industrial Revolution. Tailored support mechanisms, including grants, loans, venture capital, and crowdfunding platforms, should be made available to empower SMEs to pursue innovative initiatives.

By strategically embracing digital transformation, fostering innovation, nurturing collaborations, upskilling employees, prioritizing cybersecurity, and ensuring access to finance, SMEs can not only navigate but also leverage the Fourth Industrial Revolution for growth, enhanced competitiveness, and the creation of sustainable business models. Through these strategic initiatives, SMEs can emerge as key drivers of economic development, contributing to a prosperous and inclusive digital future.

13

Team Dynamics
Cultivating Strength, Agility &Innovation

Building strong and agile teams is crucial for the success of both SMEs and startups. In today's competitive environment team have to quickly adjust to changes, work together to collaborate and get results. For SMEs and startups operating in the digital knowledge economy within the context of the new normal and multiculturalism, building strong and agile teams is not just a strategic choice; it is a necessity for sustained growth and competitiveness.

In the context of the knowledge economy, where diversity and multiculturalism thrive, the importance of building strong and agile teams becomes even more pronounced for SMEs and startups.

In the realm of organizational success, the significance of constructing robust and adaptable teams cannot be overstated. Whether within the dynamic environment of startups or the intricate workings of established enterprises, the capability to foster teams that are both strong and agile stands as a cornerstone for achieving unparalleled success. The essence of a strong and agile team lies in its ability to not only withstand the challenges presented by a rapidly changing landscape but also to seamlessly adapt and thrive in such conditions. These teams are not just resilient; they are proactive in embracing change, leveraging it as a catalyst for innovation and progress.

The pivotal characteristic of such teams is their effective collaboration, where individual strengths are harnessed synergistically to create a collective force that is greater than the sum of its parts. Collaboration fosters a culture of open communication, idea exchange, and mutual support, enabling team members to pool their diverse skills and perspectives to solve complex problems. In the fast-paced and competitive business environment, the ability to collaborate efficiently is a key differentiator.

Furthermore, strong and agile teams consistently deliver high-performance results. Their adaptability allows them to navigate through uncertainty with confidence, turning challenges into opportunities. This adaptability is not just a reaction to change; it is a proactive approach that empowers teams to stay ahead of the curve and lead innovation in their respective domains.

In the exploration of building strong and agile teams, it becomes evident that it is not solely about assembling a group of talented individuals but rather about creating a cohesive unit with shared goals, values, and a collective commitment to excellence. The strategies and practices employed in nurturing such teams encompass leadership that fosters a culture of trust, continuous learning, and empowerment.

Adaptability to Technological Changes

In the fast-evolving digital landscape, SMEs and startups find themselves amid constant technological changes. The ability of a team to adapt swiftly to these changes is crucial for maintaining competitiveness and relevance.

Technological advancements, whether in software, hardware, or digital processes, can redefine industries and business models. Strong and agile teams understand the imperative of staying current with the latest technologies and are proactive in embracing innovation.

Adapting to technological changes involves not only the integration of new tools but also a cultural openness to evolving work practices. These teams cultivate a mindset that sees technological disruptions not as obstacles but as opportunities for growth and improvement. For instance, the adoption of cloud computing, artificial intelligence, or automation may reshape how tasks are performed and services delivered. Strong teams navigate these shifts seamlessly, ensuring that technological changes are harnessed to enhance operational efficiency and effectiveness.

Moreover, adaptability to technological changes requires continuous learning. Team members need to engage in ongoing skill development, attending workshops, online courses, and staying informed about industry trends. This commitment to learning ensures that the team remains at the forefront of technological advancements, positioning the SME or startup to respond effectively to the evolving demands of the digital landscape.

Digital Literacy

Digital literacy is the cornerstone of a team's ability to harness the full potential of the digital age. In the context of SMEs and startups, team members must go beyond basic computer skills and possess a comprehensive understanding of digital platforms, data analytics, and emerging technologies. Digital literacy encompasses the capacity to navigate digital tools effectively, interpret data insights, and leverage technology to enhance overall productivity and competitiveness.

Team members need to be adept at using a variety of digital platforms that facilitate communication, collaboration, and project management. Proficiency in data analytics is essential for making informed business decisions based on data-driven insights.

Understanding emerging technologies allows teams to explore innovative solutions, potentially disrupting traditional business models in favor of more efficient and effective approaches.

Furthermore, digital literacy promotes a culture of experimentation and innovation within the team. Team members confident in their digital skills are more likely to propose and implement creative solutions to challenges.

SMEs and startups benefit from a digitally literate workforce that can capitalize on the opportunities presented by technological advancements, ensuring a forward-looking approach to business operations.

The emergence of the new normal, marked by a significant shift towards remote work and flexible arrangements, underscores the need for teams in SMEs and startups to excel in virtual collaboration. Building strong teams in this context goes beyond mere technological proficiency; it involves fostering a culture that not only accommodates but thrives in remote settings. Teams should be equipped not just with the right collaboration tools but also with a mindset that values effective communication, trust, and accountability in virtual environments.

A key aspect of remote collaboration is the strategic use of digital communication platforms, project management tools, and virtual meeting spaces. Strong teams understand the importance of selecting and utilizing these tools effectively to maintain seamless communication and coordination.

Clear communication channels, regular check-ins, and collaborative spaces contribute to a cohesive and productive virtual work environment. Moreover, cultivating a sense of team identity and camaraderie despite physical distance is essential to boost morale and foster a shared commitment to goals.

Flexibility is a cornerstone of this adaptation. Strong teams recognize that flexibility extends beyond just working hours; it encompasses an understanding of diverse time zones, individual work preferences, and the ability to accommodate various personal and professional commitments. By embracing flexibility, teams can optimize their workflow, enhance work-life balance, and, ultimately, contribute to higher job satisfaction and performance.

Resilience and Change Management

In the face of uncertainties, strong teams in SMEs and startups must demonstrate resilience and effective change management skills. Resilience involves the ability to bounce back from challenges, setbacks, or unexpected disruptions.

Teams need to develop a mindset that views challenges not as roadblocks but as opportunities for growth and innovation. This resilience is particularly crucial in the context of the dynamic and unpredictable nature of the business landscape. Change management skills come into play when adapting to new work structures, technologies, or environmental shifts. Strong teams are proactive in anticipating and managing change, ensuring a smooth transition and minimizing potential disruptions.

Effective change management involves clear communication of the reasons behind the change, providing necessary training and support, and encouraging a positive attitude towards the evolving work landscape.

Additionally, fostering a culture of continuous improvement contributes to a team's resilience. This involves regular reflections on processes, identifying areas for enhancement, and embracing a mindset that welcomes change as a constant in the pursuit of excellence.

By instilling resilience and effective change management practices, teams can not only weather uncertainties but also position themselves to thrive and innovate in the face of evolving business conditions.

Diversity & Cultural Intelligence

Embracing multiculturalism is not just a social responsibility but a strategic advantage for SMEs and startups. Strong teams recognize the importance of creating diverse and inclusive environments.

This involves intentionally forming teams that consist of individuals from various cultural backgrounds, ethnicities, genders, and experiences. By doing so, teams tap into a rich tapestry of perspectives, fostering creativity, innovation, and a more holistic understanding of the market and customer base.

Building on diversity, strong teams prioritize the development of cultural intelligence. This goes beyond acknowledging differences; it involves actively learning about and appreciating various cultural norms, communication styles, and working practices.

Team members need to be adept at navigating cultural nuances, ensuring effective communication and collaboration. Cultural intelligence enhances teamwork by fostering a sense of belonging and creating an environment where everyone feels valued and understood.

Collaborative Learning and Knowledge Sharing
Continuous Learning Culture: In the digital knowledge economy, where information evolves rapidly, strong teams foster a culture of continuous learning.

This involves a collective commitment to staying updated on industry trends, technological advancements, and acquiring new skills. This culture ensures that team members remain adaptive and capable of leveraging the latest insights and innovations.

Team Dynamics

Cultivating Strength, Agility, and Innovation

DEFINE CLEAR OBJECTIVES

ROLES WITHIN THE TEAM SHOULD BE WELL-DEFINED

ENSURE THAT TEAM MEMBERS UNDERSTAND THEIR INDIVIDUAL ROLES AND RESPONSIBILITIES.

CULTIVATE A COLLABORATIVE CULTURE

EQUIP THE TEAM WITH TOOLS AND PROCESSES THAT ENABLE QUICK ADAPTATION TO CHANGES

FOSTER AN ENVIRONMENT WHERE INNOVATIVE IDEAS ARE VALUED

ENCOURAGE TEAM MEMBERS TO STAY UPDATED ON INDUSTRY TRENDS AND EMERGING TECHNOLOGIES

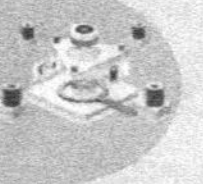

FOSTER A CULTURE OF TRUST, RESPECT, AND INCLUSIVITY

LEADERS SHOULD LEAD BY EXAMPLE

ENCOURAGE A MINDSET OF FLEXIBILITY AND RESILIENCE

Knowledge Sharing Platforms

To facilitate continuous learning, strong teams establish knowledge sharing platforms. These platforms serve as hubs for seamless sharing of insights, best practices, and lessons learned. By creating mechanisms for knowledge exchange, teams harness the collective intelligence of the group, driving innovation and efficiency.

This collaborative learning approach empowers individuals to contribute their expertise while benefiting from the collective wisdom of the team.

Innovation and Creativity

Encouraging Idea Generation: In the digital economy, innovation is a linchpin for success. Strong teams actively encourage and value idea generation from all members. Creating an environment where every team member feels empowered to contribute fosters a culture of creativity. This culture is the breeding ground for breakthrough solutions, ensuring the team remains at the forefront of industry advancements.

Agile Problem-Solving

Agile teams excel in quick and effective problem-solving. Strong teams instill a mindset that views challenges not as obstacles but as opportunities for innovation and process improvement. By embracing an agile problem-solving approach, teams can swiftly adapt to changing circumstances, turning potential setbacks into avenues for growth.

Building strong and agile teams involves a combination of effective leadership, clear communication, skill diversification, and a commitment to continuous improvement. The roles within the team should be well-defined, and the importance of these teams for enterprises and startups cannot be overstated, as they contribute to adaptability, productivity, innovation, and overall business success.

14

Strategic Brand Building

Building a strong brand is crucial for enterprises as it influences how customers perceive and interact with the business. It goes beyond just a logo; it encompasses the entire experience and values associated with the company. Establishing a robust brand presence is paramount for enterprises, as it plays a pivotal role in shaping customer perceptions and interactions with the business. More than merely a visual emblem, a strong brand extends far beyond a logo; it encapsulates the entirety of the customer experience and the core values associated with the company.

Building a strong brand is crucial for enterprises as it influences how customers perceive and interact with the business. It goes beyond just a logo; it encompasses the entire experience and values associated with the company.

Establishing a robust brand presence is paramount for enterprises, as it plays a pivotal role in shaping customer perceptions and interactions with the business. More than merely a visual emblem, a strong brand extends far beyond a logo; it encapsulates the entirety of the customer experience and the core values associated with the company. A compelling brand not only distinguishes a business from its competitors but also fosters trust and loyalty among its target audience.

The foundation of effective branding lies in a thorough understanding of the target market and aligning the brand with the aspirations and preferences of the customer base. It involves creating a distinctive identity that resonates with the values and mission of the enterprise. This identity serves as a guiding beacon, influencing not just external perceptions but also shaping internal culture and employee engagement.

Several key elements contribute to the success of a brand strategy. Consistent visual elements, such as logos, color schemes, and design aesthetics, create a cohesive and recognizable brand image. However, the brand experience is not limited to visuals; it extends to every touchpoint a customer has with the company, encompassing customer service, product quality, and overall user experience.

Effective brand building requires a strategic approach that considers both short-term and long-term objectives. A well-defined brand strategy outlines the unique value propositions, positioning in the market, and the emotional connection the brand aims to establish with its audience. This strategy serves as a roadmap for consistent brand communication and ensures that every interaction reinforces the desired brand image.

Communication is a linchpin in brand development. From advertising and marketing campaigns to social media presence, enterprises need to convey a cohesive and compelling narrative. Clear and authentic communication fosters trust and transparency, key components in building a strong brand reputation.

Establishing a robust brand identity and core values is pivotal for success. Your brand identity, spanning from mission to visual elements and voice, defines your enterprises' essence and distinguishes it in the market.

To craft this identity Clarify Mission and Vision:

Craft a mission statement capturing your venture's purpose, addressing why it exists and the problems it solves. Develop a vision statement outlining long-term goals and aspirations.

Define Core Values:
Identify guiding principles shaping your venture's culture, aligning with the mission and vision. Ensure these values permeate all aspects of your operations.

Shape Brand Personality:
Create human-like traits for your brand, influencing the tone and communication style. Align these traits with your target audience's values for resonance.

Craft Brand Positioning:
Analyze target audience, competitors, and industry trends to find a unique market position, setting your enterprise apart.

Create a Distinctive Brand Visual Identity:
• Logo: Design a memorable and versatile logo that represents your brand.
• Color Palette and Typography: Choose a consistent color scheme and font style for all brand materials.

- Imagery and Graphics: Develop a unique visual style for graphics and images associated with your brand.

Establish Consistent Branding Across Platforms:

- Website: Ensure your website reflects your brand identity in terms of design and content.
- Social Media: Maintain a consistent tone, visuals, and messaging across all social media platforms.

Print and Digital Collateral: Use a unified design approach for business cards, brochures, and other marketing materials

Brand Messaging

Brand messaging communicates your brand's value proposition using words and phrases that reflect its personality and tone. This establishes brand positioning, crucial for customer recognition. Taking a brand personality test is key in this identity-building process.

Your messaging, spanning verbal and non-verbal communication, articulates what your brand offers, why it's unique, and why customers should choose it. Importantly, this messaging is not just external but internal, ingrained in your company's values and culture.

Developing a robust brand message involves

aligning these two areas for a cohesive narrative that resonates with both your team and your audience.

External Brand Messaging:

External brand messaging involves carefully crafting words and phrases that convey the unique value proposition of your brand to the target audience. This includes defining your brand personality and ensuring that your tone of voice aligns with it. Through verbal and non-verbal communication methods, your messaging communicates what your brand does, the products or services you offer, and why your audience should choose you over competitors. This is a crucial aspect of determining your brand positioning in the market.

Internal Brand Messaging

Internally, brand messaging extends beyond external communication to become ingrained in your company's values, culture, and mission statement. It shapes how your team perceives and presents the brand. By aligning internal and external messaging, you ensure consistency in the way your customers experience both your products or services and your team. This internal cohesion contributes to a unified and authentic brand image, reinforcing the values that define your company's identity. Developing a solid brand message involves harmonizing these two main areas to create a compelling and consistent narrative that resonates with both your internal team and external audience.

Strategic Content Marketing for Branding:

Blog Posts, Articles, and Videos:

Leverage blog posts, articles, and videos as powerful tools to reinforce your brand's identity. Craft content that not only aligns with your brand values but also provides valuable information to your target audience. By consistently delivering relevant and engaging content, you establish your brand as an authoritative source within your industry. This not only aids in shaping a positive perception but also attracts and retains a loyal audience, contributing to a robust brand presence.

Storytelling:

Integrate storytelling seamlessly into your content strategy to humanize your brand. Share compelling narratives that resonate with your audience emotionally. Storytelling not only adds a personal touch but also reinforces your brand message, making it more memorable. By creating a narrative that aligns with your brand values, you foster a deeper connection with your audience. This emotional bond not only differentiates your brand in a competitive market but also enhances the overall brand experience, strengthening brand loyalty and advocacy. Incorporating storytelling into your marketing efforts ensures that your brand remains not just a product or service but a relatable and meaningful part of your audience's lives.

Strategic Evaluation and Evolution in Branding: Metrics and Analytics:

Rigorously establish key performance indicators (KPIs) to quantitatively measure the success and impact of your branding efforts. Utilize metrics and analytics tools to gauge the effectiveness of various brand elements, from online engagement to customer conversions. This data-driven approach provides valuable insights into what resonates with your audience, enabling informed decision-making and targeted improvements.

Adaptation

Embrace a culture of continuous evolution in your brand strategy. Regularly assess performance metrics and stay attuned to market dynamics. When faced with changes in consumer behavior, industry trends, or competitive landscapes, be agile in adapting your branding approach. This proactive stance ensures that your brand remains relevant, resonant, and aligned with the evolving needs and expectations of your audience. By staying adaptable, you position your brand for sustained success in a dynamic and competitive market.

By combining these strategies, enterprises can build a strong and resilient brand that resonates with their target audience, fosters trust, and creates long-lasting customer relationships. Regularly reassess and refine your brand strategy to stay relevant in a dynamic business environment.

Some tools

Building and managing a brand involves utilizing various tools across different aspects of brand development, communication, and analysis. Here are some essential tools for branding and brand building:

1. Design Tools:
- Adobe Creative Cloud: Tools like Photoshop, Illustrator, and InDesign are invaluable for creating logos, graphics, and other visual assets.
- Canva: A user-friendly platform for creating graphics, presentations, social media posts, and more, with pre-designed templates.

2. Social Media Management:
- Hootsuite or Buffer: Schedule and manage social media posts across multiple platforms, maintaining a consistent brand presence.

- Sprout Social: Provides social listening, engagement, and analytics tools for understanding and improving social media performance.

3. Content Creation and Marketing:
- HubSpot Content Strategy Tool: Helps in planning and organizing content creation aligned with your brand strategy.
- Grammarly: Ensures that all written content aligns with your brand's tone and voice.

4. Website Development:

- WordPress: A versatile and widely used platform for building and managing websites with various themes and plugins.
- Wix or Squarespace: User-friendly website builders suitable for those without extensive technical knowledge.

5. Brand Monitoring and Analytics:

- Google Analytics: Provides insights into website traffic, user behavior, and the effectiveness of online marketing efforts.
- Brandwatch: Monitors online mentions and sentiment, helping you understand how your brand is perceived.

6. Customer Relationship Management (CRM):
- Salesforce or HubSpot CRM: Helps

manage customer interactions, track leads, and maintain a database of customer information.

7. Email Marketing:
• Mailchimp or Constant Contact: Tools for designing and managing email campaigns, newsletters, and automated workflows.

8. Survey and Feedback Tools:
• SurveyMonkey or Typeform: Collect feedback and conduct surveys to understand customer perceptions and preferences.

9. Project Management:

• Trello or Asana: Organize and manage branding projects, collaborations, and timelines effectively.

10. Internal Communication:
• Slack or Microsoft Teams: Facilitate seamless communication and collaboration among team members, ensuring brand consistency.

11. Competitor Analysis:
• SEMrush or Ahrefs: Analyze competitor websites, keywords, and backlink strategies to inform your own brand strategy.

12. Legal Protection:
• Trademarkia or LegalZoom: Research and register trademarks to protect your brand legally.

13. Presentation Tools:

•   Microsoft PowerPoint or Google Slides: Create visually appealing presentations to communicate your brand story and strategy.

14. Collaboration Tools:
•   Google Workspace or Microsoft 365: Facilitate collaboration on documents, spreadsheets, and presentations within your team.

15. Brand Guidelines Tools:

•   Frontify or Bynder: Create and manage comprehensive brand guidelines, ensuring consistency in visual and messaging elements.

16. Customer Support:
•   Zendesk or Freshdesk: Provide efficient customer support and track customer interactions to maintain a positive brand image.

These tools, when used strategically, can significantly contribute to the successful development, management, and communication of your brand. Keep in mind that the specific tools you choose should align with your brand's needs, scale, and the nature of your business.

15

Business Development

Business Development (BD) is a set of activities and processes that organizations undertake to create and implement growth opportunities. It involves the pursuit of strategies to expand the business, increase revenue, and enhance overall profitability. Business Development can encompass a wide range of activities, and its focus often goes beyond immediate sales to include long-term value creation.

Business Development (BD) is a set of activities and processes that organizations undertake to create and implement growth opportunities. It involves the pursuit of strategies to expand the business, increase revenue, and enhance overall profitability. Business Development can encompass a wide range of activities, and its focus often goes beyond immediate sales to include long-term value creation.

Key aspects of Business Development include:
• Identifying Opportunities: Business Development professionals are responsible for identifying new opportunities for growth. This involves market research, trend analysis, and staying informed about industry developments.

• Building Strategic Partnerships: Developing relationships and partnerships with other businesses, organizations, or key stakeholders is a common aspect of business development. Strategic alliances can provide access to new markets, technologies, or resources.

• Market Expansion: Business Development involves strategies to enter new markets, either geographically or by targeting different customer segments. This may include international expansion, regional growth, or diversification.
• Product and Service Innovation: Constantly seeking ways to improve or create new

products and services is a crucial part of business development. This innovation can help a company stay competitive and meet the evolving needs of customers.

•	Customer Relationship Management (CRM): Building and maintaining strong relationships with customers is essential for sustainable growth. Business Development often includes efforts to enhance customer satisfaction, loyalty, and retention.

•	Sales and Revenue Generation: While distinct from sales, Business Development activities contribute to revenue generation. This could involve identifying and pursuing new sales channels, pricing strategies, or upselling and cross-selling opportunities.

•	Strategic Planning: Business Development requires a strategic approach. This involves setting goals, developing plans, and aligning resources to achieve growth objectives.

•	Negotiation and Deal Making: Negotiating and closing deals, whether with clients, partners, or suppliers, is a critical skill in business development. This may include pricing agreements, contractual partnerships, or mergers and acquisitions.

•	Risk Management: Assessing and managing risks is an integral part of business development. This includes evaluating potential challenges and uncertainties associated with new opportunities and taking steps to mitigate those risks.

• Networking and Relationship Building: Building a strong professional network is crucial in business development. This network can provide valuable insights, partnerships, and opportunities for collaboration.

Business Development is not limited to a specific industry or company size; it is applicable to enterprises of all scales, including startups, small and medium-sized enterprises (SMEs), and large corporations. The primary goal is to create sustainable value by strategically positioning the organization in the market, fostering growth, and adapting to changing business environments. Business Development professionals play a pivotal role in driving the strategic vision and long-term success of a company.

Business development strategies play a vital role in the success and growth of enterprises, startups, and small to medium-sized enterprises (SMEs). These strategies encompass a set of planned and purposeful actions aimed at creating and expanding business opportunities, increasing market share, and ensuring long-term sustainability. Here are key reasons why business development strategies are crucial:

•	Driving Growth: Business development strategies are designed to identify and capitalize on growth opportunities. This could involve entering new markets, launching new products or services, or expanding the customer base. By strategically pursuing growth, companies can increase their revenue and market presence.

•	Expanding Market Share: Effective business development strategies help organizations gain a competitive edge and capture a larger share of the market. This might involve market research to identify untapped segments, developing unique value propositions, or establishing strategic partnerships to enhance market presence.

•	Building Sustainable Success: Sustainability is a key consideration for long-term success. Business development strategies should focus not only on short-term gains but also on creating a foundation for sustainable growth. This may involve building strong customer relationships, investing in innovation, and adapting to changing market conditions.

•	Diversification: Diversifying the business portfolio is often a crucial aspect of business development. Companies may explore new product lines, target different customer segments, or enter adjacent markets. Diversification helps mitigate risks and opens up new avenues for revenue generation.

•	Strategic Partnerships and Alliances: Collaborations with other businesses can be a powerful business development strategy. Strategic partnerships, alliances, and collaborations can provide access to new markets, technologies, and resources, fostering mutual growth and success.

•	Adapting to Market Trends: Business development strategies should be dynamic and responsive to market trends. Staying informed about industry changes, consumer preferences, and technological advancements allows companies to adapt their strategies to remain relevant and competitive.

•	Effective Marketing and Branding: Developing a strong brand presence and implementing effective marketing strategies are integral to business development. This involves creating a compelling brand identity, understanding the target audience, and implementing marketing campaigns that resonate with customers.

•	Customer-Centric Approach: Prioritizing the needs and preferences of customers is essential for sustained success. Business development strategies should include a customer-centric approach, focusing on delivering value and creating positive customer experiences to build loyalty and advocacy.

•   Investing in Innovation: To stay ahead in competitive markets, businesses must embrace innovation. This could involve developing new products, adopting cutting-edge technologies, or finding creative solutions to existing challenges. Innovation is often a key driver of business development and growth.

•   Global Expansion: For enterprises with global aspirations, business development strategies may include expanding operations internationally. This requires careful consideration of cultural, regulatory, and market differences, as well as effective global marketing and distribution strategies.

In summary, business development strategies are essential for enterprises, startups, and SMEs to navigate the dynamic business landscape, identify growth opportunities, and build a resilient foundation for long-term success. These strategies involve a combination of market analysis, strategic planning, and effective execution to drive growth, increase market share, and ensure sustainable business success.

BUSINESS DEVELOPMENT IN DIGITAL ERA

In the digital era, business development has been significantly impacted by technological advancements, changing consumer behaviors, and the evolution of digital platforms. Here are some key approaches to business development in the digital era:

- Content Marketing: Creating and distributing valuable, relevant content to attract and engage a target audience. This includes blogs, videos, social media posts, and other digital content.

- Search Engine Optimization (SEO): Optimizing online content to improve search engine rankings and increase visibility in search results.

- Social Media Marketing: Leveraging social media platforms to build brand awareness, engage with audiences, and drive traffic to websites.

- Email Marketing: Utilizing email campaigns to nurture leads, communicate with customers, and promote products or services.

In the digital era, successful business development requires a proactive approach to leveraging technology, embracing innovation, and staying agile in response to evolving market dynamics.

Digital tools and strategies should be integrated seamlessly into business operations to unlock growth opportunities and foster long-term success

16

Digital Era Marketing

In a digitally driven economy, marketing has undergone significant transformations, offering numerous potentials and opportunities for businesses looking to expand their market horizons.Marketing in a digitally driven economy demands a holistic approach that integrates technology, data-driven insights, and a keen understanding of consumer behavior. Embracing the transformative power of digital marketing opens the door to unparalleled opportunities for businesses to thrive and grow in an increasingly interconnected and technologically advanced marketplace.

In the dynamic landscape of a digitally driven economy, marketing has evolved into a multifaceted and technologically infused discipline, presenting businesses with unprecedented opportunities for growth and innovation. As traditional marketing methods give way to digital strategies, organizations must adapt to stay relevant and capitalize on the expansive reach and engagement potential of the online realm.

One of the paramount aspects to consider in this digital era is the omnipresence of technology and the internet. With an increasing number of consumers relying on digital platforms for information, entertainment, and commerce, businesses must establish a robust online presence. This involves not only creating user-friendly websites but also optimizing for search engines (SEO) to enhance visibility in a vast online landscape.

Social media platforms play a pivotal role in shaping consumer behavior and preferences. Marketing strategies need to incorporate targeted and engaging social media campaigns to connect with the audience on platforms like Facebook, Instagram, Twitter, and LinkedIn. Leveraging the power of influencers and user-generated content can amplify brand reach and foster a sense of community, enhancing the overall effectiveness of digital marketing efforts.

Data-driven decision-making has become a cornerstone of successful marketing in the digitally driven economy. Businesses can harness the wealth of data available to analyze consumer behavior, preferences, and trends. This data-driven approach enables the creation of personalized and targeted marketing campaigns, ensuring that businesses can tailor their messaging to specific audience segments for maximum impact.

The advent of artificial intelligence (AI) and machine learning has further revolutionized marketing strategies. These technologies can analyze vast datasets, predict consumer behavior, and automate various aspects of marketing, such as chatbots for customer service and programmatic advertising for real-time ad placements. Embracing AI-driven tools empowers businesses to streamline processes, enhance efficiency, and deliver a more personalized and responsive customer experience.

E-commerce has become an integral part of the digitally driven economy, and businesses must optimize their online sales channels. This involves creating seamless and secure online purchasing experiences, implementing effective payment gateways, and leveraging e-commerce platforms to their full potential. Additionally, mobile optimization is crucial, as a significant portion of digital interactions and transactions now occurs on smartphones and tablets.

Agility and adaptability are paramount in the face of rapidly evolving digital trends. Marketing strategies need to be flexible, allowing businesses to pivot quickly in response to changes in consumer behavior, emerging technologies, or market dynamics. Continuous monitoring of key performance indicators (KPIs) and staying attuned to industry trends will enable businesses to stay ahead of the curve and make informed marketing decisions.

Marketing in a digitally driven economy demands a holistic approach that integrates technology, data-driven insights, and a keen understanding of consumer behavior. Embracing the transformative power of digital marketing opens the door to unparalleled opportunities for businesses to thrive and grow in an increasingly interconnected and technologically advanced marketplace.

Potentials and Opportunities in Digital Marketing

Global Reach

•	Digital marketing allows businesses to reach a global audience without the constraints of traditional geographical boundaries.
•	Online platforms enable the expansion of market horizons to international markets.

Data-Driven Insights:
•	The abundance of data available through digital channels provides valuable insights into consumer behavior.
•	Businesses can leverage analytics to understand customer preferences, optimize marketing strategies, and personalize campaigns.
Targeted Advertising:
•	Digital platforms enable precise targeting based on demographics, interests, and online behavior.
•	This allows businesses to tailor their marketing messages to specific segments, increasing the relevance of their campaigns.
Social Media Engagement:
•	Social media platforms offer opportunities for direct engagement with the audience.
•	Businesses can build brand awareness, foster customer relationships, and leverage user-generated content for marketing.

E-commerce Integration:
•	Digital marketing seamlessly integrates with e-commerce platforms, providing a direct path from marketing efforts to online sales.
•	Businesses can capitalize on the growing trend of online shopping and create seamless customer journeys.
Content Marketing and SEO:
•	Quality content remains a key driver in digital marketing success.

• Investing in content marketing and optimizing for search engines enhances online visibility, driving organic traffic.

Mobile Marketing:

• With the increasing use of mobile devices, mobile marketing offers new avenues for reaching consumers on-the-go.
• Mobile apps, SMS marketing, and location-based services contribute to a more personalized and immediate connection with the audience.

Emerging Technologies:

• Innovations such as augmented reality (AR), virtual reality (VR), and voice search present new opportunities for creative and immersive marketing experiences.
• Businesses can explore these technologies to stand out in a crowded digital landscape.

Personalization and Customer Experience:

• Digital marketing allows for highly personalized campaigns based on user preferences and behaviors.
• Enhancing the overall customer experience through personalized content and targeted messaging can build brand loyalty.

Performance Measurement:

•	Digital marketing provides real-time performance metrics.
•	Businesses can analyze the effectiveness of campaigns promptly and make data-driven adjustments to optimize ROI.

Collaborations and Influencer Marketing:

•	Partnering with influencers and collaborating with other businesses in the digital space can broaden an enterprise's market reach.

•	Influencer marketing can provide access to niche audiences and build credibility.

Strategies for Expanding Market Horizons:

International SEO:

•	Optimize digital content for international search engines to reach a global audience.

Localized Content:

•	Tailor content to specific cultural nuances and languages to resonate with diverse audiences.

Cross-Channel Marketing:

•	Integrate marketing efforts across multiple digital channels for a cohesive and omnichannel experience.

Social Listening:

•	Utilize social listening tools to understand market trends and consumer sentiments globally.

Adaptation to Emerging Markets:

•	Stay abreast of emerging markets and adapt marketing strategies to fit local contexts and preferences.

E-commerce Localization:

•	Localize e-commerce platforms, payment methods, and product offerings to cater to diverse markets.

Collaborative Partnerships:

•	Forge partnerships with local businesses or influencers to gain credibility and trust in new markets.

Agile Marketing

- Embrace agile marketing methodologies to quickly adapt to changing market dynamics and consumer behaviors.

The digitally driven economy offers vast potentials for businesses to expand their market horizons. Leveraging data, targeting capabilities, and emerging technologies, along with strategic adaptations for global reach, can position businesses for success in the dynamic landscape of digital marketing.

17

Effective Sales Pitch

An effective sales pitch is a crucial tool for persuading potential customers to engage with your product or service. It's a carefully crafted message that communicates the unique value and benefits of what you're offering.

A successful sales pitch is a strategic communication tool that combines audience understanding, a compelling introduction, benefits-focused messaging, storytelling, rapport-building, objection handling, urgency creation, and a clear call to action.

Creating an effective sales pitch involves a combination of understanding your audience, addressing their needs, and presenting your product or service in a compelling way.

An effective sales pitch is a crucial tool for persuading potential customers to engage with your product or service. It's a carefully crafted message that communicates the unique value and benefits of what you're offering. Whether you're selling a physical product, a service, or an idea, a well-structured sales pitch can capture attention, build rapport, and ultimately drive the desired action from your audience.

To create a compelling sales pitch, it's essential to understand your target audience thoroughly. This involves researching their needs, challenges, and preferences. By tailoring your pitch to address specific pain points and desires, you can increase the relevance of your message and resonate more strongly with potential customers.

The introduction of your sales pitch is a critical component. You want to grab your audience's attention right from the start. This could involve using a compelling hook, sharing a relevant statistic, or posing a thought-provoking question. Clearly stating the purpose of your pitch and explaining how your product or service can solve a problem or fulfill a need is essential in setting the stage for the rest of your presentation. Throughout the pitch, it's crucial to focus on the benefits your offering provides rather than just listing features. Customers are more interested in understanding how a product or service will improve their lives or solve their problems. Using storytelling techniques can also be powerful, as narratives tend to stick with people and create a more emotional connection to your message.

Building rapport with your audience is another key aspect of a successful sales pitch. Finding common ground, showing genuine interest, and using open-ended questions can help establish a connection. This connection lays the foundation for trust and makes the prospect more receptive to your message.

Anticipating and addressing objections is a proactive strategy in a sales pitch. By acknowledging and overcoming potential concerns, you demonstrate a deep understanding of your customer's perspective and build credibility. Additionally, creating a sense of urgency and providing a clear call to action at the end of your pitch can encourage immediate decision-making and action.

Remember that a concise, well-organized pitch is more likely to keep your audience engaged. Visual aids, such as slides or demonstrations, can enhance understanding and retention of information. Lastly, practice and refinement are essential. The more familiar and comfortable you become with your pitch, the more confidently you can deliver it in real-world situations.

A successful sales pitch is a strategic communication tool that combines audience understanding, a compelling introduction, benefits-focused messaging, storytelling, rapport-building, objection handling, urgency creation, and a clear call to action. Through continuous practice and adaptation, you can refine your pitch to effectively engage and persuade your target audience.

Here are some key steps to help you craft a successful sales pitch:

Know Your Audience:
•	Understand the needs, challenges, and interests of your target audience.
•	Tailor your pitch to resonate with their specific pain points and desires.

Start with a Strong Introduction:
•	Capture attention from the beginning with a compelling hook or a relevant statistic.
•	Clearly state the purpose of your pitch and how your product or service can benefit the prospect.

- Highlight the value and benefits your product or service brings to the customer.
- Explain how it solves their problems or improves their situation.

Build Rapport:

- Establish a connection by finding common ground or showing genuine interest in the prospect.
- Use open-ended questions to encourage engagement and understanding of their needs.

Use Storytelling:

- Share success stories or case studies that demonstrate how your product/service has helped others.
- People often connect with narratives, making your pitch more memorable.

Address Objections Proactively:

- Anticipate potential concerns or objections the prospect might have and address them during your pitch.
- Be prepared to provide evidence or solutions to overcome objections.

Create a Sense of Urgency:

- Encourage action by creating a sense of urgency or highlighting limited-time offers.
- Convey the benefits of acting now rather than later.

Keep it Concise:

• Focus on the key points and avoid overwhelming the prospect with too much information.

• Aim for a pitch that can be delivered in a relatively short amount of time.

Utilize Visuals:

• Use visuals like slides, charts, or demonstrations to enhance your message and make it more memorable.

• Visual aids can help clarify complex information and keep the prospect engaged.

End with a Clear Call to Action (CTA):

• Clearly state what you want the prospect to do next.

• Whether it's making a purchase, scheduling a demo, or signing up for a trial, make the next steps explicit.

Practice and Refine:

• Practice your pitch to ensure smooth delivery and confidence.

• Seek feedback and be willing to refine your pitch based on the responses you receive.

Remember, adaptability is key. Pay attention to the prospect's reactions and adjust your pitch accordingly. Tailoring your approach based on the specific needs and preferences of your audience will increase your chances of making a successful sale.

18

Effective Pitch Deck

A pitch deck is a pitch presentation for entrepreneurs or businesses to provide a streamlined but informative overview of their company or startup to potential investors, such as venture capitalists or angel investors. clients or investors to work with them.

An effective pitch deck is a concise and compelling presentation that conveys key information about your business, value proposition, market opportunity, and financials to potential investors or stakeholders. It serves as a visual aid to support your oral presentation and is a critical tool for attracting interest and funding.

What is an effective PITCH DECK

Pitch decks, also known as marketing decks, are primarily used by businesses trying to convince
In the context of startups, a pitch deck is a pitch presentation for entrepreneurs or businesses to provide a streamlined but informative overview of their company or startup to potential investors, such as venture capitalists or angel investors. clients or investors to work with them.

An effective pitch deck is a concise and compelling presentation that conveys key information about your business, value proposition, market opportunity, and financials to potential investors or stakeholders. It serves as a visual aid to support your oral presentation and is a critical tool for attracting interest and funding.

Creating an effective pitch deck is crucial for presenting your business or startup to potential investors, partners, or stakeholders. A pitch deck typically includes key information about your business, value proposition, market opportunity, financials, and team. Here's a guide on how to create a compelling pitch deck:

Startup PITCH DECK

A startup pitch deck is a brief presentation that provides investors with an overview of your new business and/or startup idea through presentation slides. It usually focuses on showcasing your product, sharing your business model, giving a look into your monetization strategy, and introducing your team

Structure of a Pitch Deck:

Introduction
•	Title Slide: Company name, logo, and a tagline.
•	Mission Statement: A brief overview of your company's mission.
Problem and Solution
•	Problem Statement: Clearly articulate the problem your product or service solves.
•	Solution: Present your unique solution and value proposition.
Market Opportunity
•	Market Size: Define the target market and its size.
•	Traction: Showcase any initial success or traction in the market.
Business Model
•	Revenue Model: Explain how your business makes money.
•	Pricing Strategy: Outline your pricing structure.
Product or Service
•	Product Overview: Provide a detailed description of your product or service.

- Highlight the unique features that set your offering apart.

Market Validation

- Include quotes or testimonials from satisfied customers.
- Share success stories or case studies if applicable.

Go-to-Market Strategy

- Explain how you plan to reach your target audience.
- Outline key marketing initiatives.

Competitive Landscape

- Identify and briefly analyze key competitors.
- Clearly articulate what makes your offering superior.

Financial Projections

- Provide realistic and well-researched revenue forecasts.
- Highlight important financial metrics.

Team

- Founder/Team Introduction: Briefly introduce the key members of your team.
- Highlight relevant skills and experiences.

Funding requirement

- Clearly state the amount of funding you are seeking.
- Specify how the funds will be utilized.
- Closing and Contact Information:
- Summary Slide: Recap the key points.

*   Contact Information: Include contact details for further inquiries.

Tips for Creating a Compelling Pitch Deck

Clarity and Simplicity
*   Keep slides clear, concise, and easy to understand.
*   Use visuals, charts, and graphics to convey information.
Storytelling
*   Craft a compelling narrative that captivates your audience.
*   Tell the story of your business journey and the problem you're solving.
Visual Consistency
*   Maintain a consistent design theme throughout the pitch deck.
*   Use a professional and visually appealing layout.
Know Your Audience
*   Tailor your pitch deck to the specific needs and interests of your audience.
*   Research potential investors or partners to understand their preferences.

Other key points to remember

*   *Practice delivering your pitch with confidence and enthusiasm.*
*   *Be prepared to answer questions and address concerns.*

- *Support claims and projections with data and evidence.*

Use metrics and key performance indicators to demonstrate progress.

Highlight Achievements

- Showcase any milestones, partnerships, or awards your business has achieved.
- Provide evidence of market validation and customer interest.

Remember that a pitch deck is a visual aid to support your oral presentation.

Keep slides succinct, focus on key messages, and use the opportunity to engage your audience.

Tailor your pitch deck based on the specific requirements of the situation and the preferences of your target audience.

19

Be Your Own Brand Ambassador & Communication Strategist

Traditional advertising is no longer the sole domain of big corporations. Digital technologies like social media and e-commerce platforms have empowered entrepreneurs to reach a global audience and directly connect with their target market. Being your own brand ambassador and communication strategist in today's digital age requires a combination of creativity, strategic thinking, and proficiency in leveraging available tools and platforms. By embracing these skills and staying adaptable to emerging technologies, entrepreneurs can effectively promote their brands and thrive in an increasingly competitive market.

In today's digitally driven global market, the role of entrepreneurs and small business managers as their own brand ambassadors and communication strategists has never been more crucial.

Gone are the days when brand promotion and communication strategies were solely the domain of large corporations with hefty advertising budgets. Now, thanks to the evolution of media and communication channels, particularly through digital technologies, entrepreneurs and small business managers have unparalleled opportunities to shape their brand narratives and engage with their target audiences directly.

The rise of the internet and social media has democratized brand promotion, giving individuals and businesses of all sizes the ability to reach a global audience with relative ease. Through strategic content creation, community engagement, and influencer collaborations, entrepreneurs can build authentic relationships with their audience, fostering loyalty and trust in their brands.

The advent of e-commerce platforms and digital marketing tools has further leveled the playing field for small businesses. With the click of a button, entrepreneurs can set up online storefronts, launch targeted advertising campaigns, and track the effectiveness of their marketing efforts in real-time. This data-driven approach to brand promotion enables entrepreneurs to optimize their strategies, refine their messaging, and adapt to changing market trends with agility.

Story telling & content marketing

In addition to traditional marketing tactics, entrepreneurs can harness the power of storytelling and content marketing to differentiate their brands in a crowded marketplace. By sharing their values, mission, and unique selling propositions through compelling narratives, entrepreneurs can resonate with their audience on a deeper emotional level, driving brand affinity and customer loyalty. In today's digitally driven global market, the role of entrepreneurs and small business managers as their own brand ambassadors and communication strategists is more critical than ever before.

Social media platforms provide a level playing field

Social media platforms have emerged as powerful tools for entrepreneurs to market and promote their brands. From creating engaging content to interacting with their audience in real-time, social media provides a level playing field where skill and creativity outweigh the need for hefty advertising budgets. By leveraging these platforms strategically, entrepreneurs can build a strong online presence, engage with their target audience, and establish themselves as thought leaders in their respective industries.
Social media enables entrepreneurs to interact

with their audience in real-time, fostering authentic connections and building trust. Through likes, comments, shares, and direct messages, entrepreneurs can engage in conversations with their followers, address their concerns, and gather valuable feedback that informs their business decisions. This two-way communication not only strengthens brand loyalty but also humanizes the brand, making it more relatable and approachable to consumers.

Social media allows entrepreneurs to showcase their expertise and establish themselves as thought leaders in their respective industries. By sharing valuable insights, industry trends, and behind-the-scenes glimpses of their business operations, entrepreneurs can position themselves as authorities in their field, attracting followers who value their expertise and perspective. This positioning not only enhances brand credibility but also opens doors to collaboration opportunities and media exposure.

Not much of financial investment but skill and knowledge intensive:

Branding and executing communication strategies no longer require substantial financial investments. With the rise of content marketing, storytelling, and influencer collaborations, entrepreneurs can craft compelling narratives that resonate with their audience without breaking the bank. Authenticity and transparency have become paramount, with consumers gravitating towards brands that share their values and beliefs.

In today's dynamic business landscape, effective communication strategies are no longer dependent on hefty financial investments, but rather on the depth of skill and knowledge possessed by entrepreneurs. The rise of content marketing, storytelling, and influencer collaborations has revolutionized the way brands communicate with their audience, allowing entrepreneurs to craft compelling narratives that resonate without draining their budgets.

Influencer collaborations

Influencer collaborations have emerged as a cost-effective way for entrepreneurs to amplify their brand reach and credibility. By partnering with influencers who share their target audience, entrepreneurs can leverage the influencer's existing following to promote their products or services authentically. Unlike traditional advertising campaigns, which often require significant financial investments, influencer collaborations can be tailored to fit any budget, making them accessible to entrepreneurs of all sizes.

Consumers are increasingly gravitating towards brands that share their values and beliefs, and are more likely to engage with content that feels genuine and authentic. By being transparent about their business practices, values, and mission, entrepreneurs can build trust and credibility with their audience, leading to long-term loyalty and advocacy.

Being your own brand ambassador and communication strategist in today's digital age requires a combination of creativity, strategic thinking, and proficiency in leveraging available tools and platforms. By embracing these skills and staying adaptable to emerging technologies, entrepreneurs can effectively promote their brands and thrive in an increasingly competitive market.

20

Finding Money for your Venture

Without adequate financing, entrepreneurs may struggle to cover initial expenses, invest in essential resources like equipment and technology, hire talented staff, or expand their business operations. Finance enables entrepreneurs to seize opportunities for growth, innovate, and navigate challenges in a competitive market. Additionally, having access to capital can provide a buffer during lean times and help sustain the business through fluctuations in revenue or unexpected expenses. Overall, finance is crucial for entrepreneurs as it fuels innovation, drives growth, and ultimately contributes to the success and sustainability of their ventures.

In today's rapidly evolving business landscape, access to financial resources is fundamental for the success and growth of small entrepreneurs, start-up ventures, and SMEs (Small and Medium Enterprises). As the business environment becomes increasingly competitive and dynamic, having the necessary funds can mean the difference between seizing opportunities for expansion and struggling to stay afloat.

Traditional Financing Options

Traditional financing options serve as foundational pillars for entrepreneurs, offering stability and reliability in accessing capital. These avenues have long been the bedrock for small businesses and startups to secure funds for various needs. Here are some key traditional financing options:

Bank Loans

- Bank loans are a common form of financing for small businesses. Entrepreneurs can approach banks to obtain loans for starting a business, purchasing equipment, expanding operations, or covering working capital needs.
- Bank loans typically require collateral, such as property or inventory, and the terms and interest rates vary based on factors like creditworthiness and the purpose of the loan.
- Small businesses can opt for different

types of bank loans, including term loans, lines of credit, or SBA (Small Business Administration) loans, which are partially guaranteed by the government to mitigate lender risk.

Government-Sponsored Programs

•	Governments often provide support to small businesses through various programs and initiatives aimed at promoting entrepreneurship and economic growth.
•	Small businesses may benefit from government-backed loans, grants, or subsidies tailored to specific industries, regions, or business objectives.
•	These programs can offer favorable terms, lower interest rates, or assistance with meeting regulatory requirements, making them attractive financing options for entrepreneurs.

Trade Credit

•	Trade credit refers to the practice of suppliers extending credit terms to small businesses, allowing them to purchase goods or services on credit and pay at a later date.
•	This form of financing helps small businesses manage cash flow by deferring payment until revenue is generated from sales.
•	Trade credit arrangements may vary in terms of payment terms, credit limits, and interest

rates, depending on the relationship between the buyer and the supplier.

Equipment Financing

- Equipment financing enables small businesses to acquire essential equipment or machinery without paying the full purchase price upfront.
- Entrepreneurs can finance equipment through loans, leases, or hire purchase agreements, spreading the cost over time while benefiting from immediate access to the necessary assets.
- Equipment financing options may offer flexibility in terms of repayment schedules and may be secured or unsecured depending on the lender's requirements.

Commercial Mortgages

- Commercial mortgages allow small business owners to purchase or refinance commercial properties, such as office buildings, warehouses, or retail spaces.
- These loans are secured by the property itself and typically offer longer repayment terms and lower interest rates compared to other types of financing.
- Commercial mortgages provide small businesses with the opportunity to own real estate assets, build equity, and establish a long-term presence in their respective industries.

Overall, traditional financing options play a crucial role in providing small businesses and entrepreneurs with the capital they need to start, grow, and sustain their ventures. While these avenues offer stability and reliability, it's essential for entrepreneurs to carefully evaluate their financing needs, consider the associated costs and risks, and choose the most suitable option based on their business objectives and financial circumstances.

Alternative finance/funding options

Alternative funding options offer innovative ways for entrepreneurs to secure capital for their ventures, often providing flexibility, accessibility, and unique opportunities for growth. Here are some key alternative funding options:

Venture Capital

- Venture capital (VC) funding is well-suited for startup ventures with high growth potential and scalable business models.
- Venture capital firms invest capital in exchange for an ownership stake in the company, typically taking an active role in guiding strategic decisions and providing expertise.
- Startups seeking venture capital funding often undergo rigorous due diligence processes and pitch presentations to demonstrate their mar-

ket potential, team capabilities, and growth prospects.

Angel Investors

•	Angel investors are affluent individuals who provide capital to early-stage startups in exchange for equity ownership or convertible debt.
•	Unlike venture capital firms, angel investors may offer more flexible terms and a more hands-on approach, often providing mentorship, networking opportunities, and industry expertise to the entrepreneurs they support.
•	Angel investors are typically drawn to innovative ideas, passionate founders, and potential for high returns on investment.

Crowdfunding

•	Crowdfunding platforms leverage the power of the crowd to raise funds for entrepreneurial ventures from a large pool of individual investors, often through online campaigns.
•	Entrepreneurs can utilize crowdfunding to finance their projects by offering rewards, equity, or pre-sales of products or services to backers.
•	Crowdfunding provides entrepreneurs with an opportunity to validate their ideas, engage with their target audience, and generate buzz around their ventures while raising capital.
Each of these alternative funding options offers

distinct advantages and considerations for entrepreneurs. Venture capital provides access to significant capital and strategic guidance but may involve giving up a portion of ownership and control. Angel investors offer more personalized support and flexibility but may have varying levels of experience and resources. Crowdfunding enables entrepreneurs to leverage community support and validation but requires effective marketing and campaign management. Ultimately, entrepreneurs should carefully evaluate their funding needs, assess the pros and cons of each option, and choose the approach that aligns best with their business goals and values.

Innovative Financing Models

Innovative financing models are reshaping the landscape of capital acquisition for entrepreneurs, offering novel approaches that cater to diverse needs and preferences. Here are three innovative financing models:

Peer-to-Peer Lending

- Peer-to-peer (P2P) lending platforms facilitate direct lending transactions between borrowers and investors, cutting out traditional financial intermediaries like banks.
- Entrepreneurs can access capital from individual investors willing to lend money at competitive interest rates, often lower than those offered by banks.
- P2P lending offers flexibility in terms of

loan amounts, repayment schedules, and eligibility criteria, making it an attractive alternative for small businesses seeking financing.

Revenue-Based Financing

• Revenue-based financing (RBF) enables entrepreneurs to raise capital by selling a percentage of future revenues to investors.
• Unlike traditional equity financing, RBF does not involve giving up ownership or control of the business. Instead, investors receive a share of the company's future revenues until a predetermined repayment cap is reached.
• RBF arrangements provide entrepreneurs with flexibility in managing cash flow, as repayments are tied to the company's performance rather than fixed monthly payments.

These innovative financing models offer entrepreneurs alternative pathways to raise capital, diversify funding sources, and access new investor pools. However, it's essential for entrepreneurs to conduct thorough due diligence, understand the associated risks, and align financing decisions with their business goals and risk tolerance. By leveraging innovative financing models responsibly, entrepreneurs can unlock new opportunities for growth and innovation in the ever-evolving landscape of entrepreneurship.

Grants and Subsidies

Grants and subsidies, along with microfinance and community development finance, serve as vital resources for small entrepreneurs and SMEs, particularly those operating in underserved communities or pursuing innovative ventures. Here's an overview of these two essential funding avenues:

● Government agencies and private organizations frequently provide grants and subsidies to support various initiatives aimed at fostering innovation, research and development (R&D), and business expansion.

● These funding opportunities are typically non-repayable and may cover a wide range of activities, including product development, market research, technology adoption, and capacity building.

● Grants and subsidies play a critical role in enabling small entrepreneurs and SMEs to undertake projects that may otherwise be financially challenging or high-risk, driving innovation, competitiveness, and economic growth.

Microfinance and Community Development Finance
● Microfinance institutions (MFIs) specialize in providing small loans and financial services to entrepreneurs, often in low-income or underserved communities where traditional banking services may be limited or inaccessible.

- Microfinance empowers individuals, particularly women and marginalized groups, to start or expand microenterprises, thereby creating economic opportunities, reducing poverty, and fostering social inclusion.
- Community development finance institutions (CDFIs) similarly focus on providing financial services and investment capital to underserved communities, supporting local businesses, affordable housing projects, and community development initiatives.
- By offering accessible and tailored financial products, microfinance and community development finance play a vital role in promoting entrepreneurship, job creation, and sustainable development at the grassroots level.

Together, grants and subsidies, along with microfinance and community development finance, contribute to building a supportive ecosystem for small entrepreneurs and SMEs, enabling them to access the capital and resources needed to thrive and make positive contributions to their communities and economies. It's essential for entrepreneurs to explore these funding options, leverage available opportunities, and strategically align their business goals with the funding sources that best meet their needs and objectives.

In today's dynamic business environment, small entrepreneurs, startup ventures, and SMEs have access to a wide range of financial resources and funding options. By leveraging traditional avenues, exploring alternative funding models, and tapping into innovative financing solutions, entrepreneurs can secure the capital needed to fuel their growth and realize their entrepreneurial ambitions. However, it's essential to carefully evaluate each funding option, consider the associated risks and benefits, and develop a strategic approach to financing that aligns with the goals and needs of the business. Ultimately, access to diverse financial resources is essential for driving innovation, fostering economic growth, and building a thriving ecosystem of entrepreneurship in the modern era.

Reading list

• Amabile, T. M. The creativity key. Harvard Business School Press. 1990.

• Blank, Steve. The Four Steps to the Epiphany: Successful Strategies for Products that Win. Wiley, 2013.

• Brown, Tim. Change by Design: How Design Thinking Transforms Organizations and Inspires Innovation, Harper Business, 2009.

• Belsky, Scott. Making Ideas Happen: Overcoming the Obstacles Between Vision and Reality. Portfolio, 2010.

• Carree, Martyn A., and Thérèse Bouma. "Research on Corporate Social Responsibility in Small and Medium-Sized Enterprises: A Review of the Literature." Journal of Business Ethics 88.3 pp. 299-316, 2009.

• Challenger, Matthew Dixon, and Brent Adamson. The Challenger Sale: Taking Control of the Conversation with Your Customers. Wiley, 2011.

• Chesbrough, Henry W. Open Innovation: The New Imperative for Creating and Profiting from Technology. Harvard Business Review Press, 2006.

•	Christensen, Clayton M. The Innovator's Dilemma: When New Technologies Cause Great Firms to Fail. Harvard Business Review Press, 2016.

•	Clercq, D., Lumpkin, G. T., & Burgelman, R. C. Managing for innovation: An organizational perspective. Pergamon. 2001

•	Csikszentmihalyi, Mihaly. Creativity: Flow and the Psychology of Discovery and Invention. Harper Perennial, 1997.

•	Deighton, John, and Leora Kornfeld. Digital Marketing Strategy: Text and Cases. Wiley, 2018.

•	Dorst, Kees. Frame Innovation: Create New Thinking by Design. MIT Press, 2015.

•	Duckworth, Angela. Grit: The Power of Passion and Perseverance. Scribner, 2016.

•	Dweck, Carol S. Mindset: The New Psychology of Success. Ballantine Books, 2007.

•	Eisenberg, Bryan, Jeffrey Eisenberg, and Lisa T. Davis. Call to Action: Secret Formulas to Improve Online Results. Thomas Nelson, 2006.

•	Evans, Dave, and Jake McKee. Social Media Marketing: An Hour a Day. Wiley, 2012.

•	Ferguson, C. Born digital: How the baby boomers changed the world and what it means for all of us. Penguin. 2012.

•	Gerber, Michael E. The E-Myth Revisited: Why Most Small Businesses Don't Work and What to Do About It. HarperCollins e-books, 2009.

• Gitomer, Jeffrey. The Sales Bible: The Ultimate Sales Resource. Wiley, 2008.

• Gladwell, Malcolm. Outliers: The Story of Success. Little, Brown and Company, 2008.

• Godin, Seth. Purple Cow: Transform Your Business by Being Remarkable. Portfolio, 2003.

• Godin, Seth. Tribes: We need you to lead us. Penguin. 2011

• Hisrich, Robert D., Michael P. Peters, and Dean A. Shepherd. Entrepreneurship. McGraw-Hill Education, 2018.

• Nir Eyal, Hooked: How to Build Habit-Forming Products.

• India Micro Small and Medium Enterprises Reports Series , India SME observatory, ISED, Kochi, Kerala.

• Kennedy, Dan S. No B.S. Sales Success in The New Economy. Entrepreneur Press, 2010.

• Koshy, P. India's entrepreneurship policy: Future tasks and vision. 2019

• Kotler, Philip, et al. Marketing 4.0: Moving from Traditional to Digital. Wiley, 2016.

• Kotler, P., & Keller, K. L. Marketing management. Pearson.2020

• Liedtka, Jeanne, Andrew King, and Kevin Bennett. Solving Problems with Design Thinking: Ten Stories of What Works. Columbia University Press, 2013.

• Longenecker, J. G., Petty, J. W., Palich, L. E., & Hoy, F. Small Business Management:

Launching & Growing Entrepre¬neurial Ventures - Softcover. Cengage Learning. 2022.
•	Lockwood, T. Design thinking: Integrating innovation, customer experience, and business strategy. John Wiley & Sons. 2010
•	Massey, Barbara Findlay, and Linda Pinson. Steps to Small Business Start-Up: Everything You Need to Know to Turn Your Idea into a Successful Business. Kaplan Business, 2005.
•	Meinel, C., & List, B. Design thinking for strategic innovation: A user-centered approach for creative problem solving. Springer. 2018.
•	Moore, Geoffrey A. Crossing the Chasm: Marketing and Selling High-Tech Products to Mainstream Customers. Harper Business, 2014.
•	Morris, Michael H., Jr. The Innovator's Solution: Creating and Sustaining Successful Growth. HarperCollins, 2011.
•	Nambisan, Satish. Digital and the Fourth Industrial Revolution. Wiley, 2017.
•	Osterwalder, Alexander, and Yves Pigneur. Business Model Generation: A Handbook for Visionaries, Game Changers, and Challengers. Wiley, 2010.
•	Pink, Daniel H. Drive: The Surprising Truth About What Motivates Us. Riverhead Books, 2011.
•	Pink, Daniel H. To Sell Is Human: The Surprising Truth About Moving Others. Riverhead Books, 2013.

•	Pinchot, III, Gifford. The Art of Innovation. Harper Perennial, 2004.

•	Ries, Eric. The Lean Startup: How Today's Entrepreneurs Use Continuous Innovation to Create Radically Successful Businesses. Currency, 2011.

•	Ries, Eric, and Beth. Startup Lessons Learned: How Everything You Think You Know About Success Is (Often) Wrong. Wiley, 2011.

•	Rainsberry, Rick, et al. Sales Growth: Five Proven Strategies from the World's Sales Leaders. Wiley, 2016.

•	Sarasvathy, Saras D. Effectuation: Elements of Entrepreneurial Expertise. Edward Elgar Publishing, 2008.

•	Schrage, Michael. Serious Play: How the World's Best Companies Simulate to Innovate. Harvard Business Review Press, 1999.

•	Stickdorn, Marc, and Jakob Schneider. This is Service Design Thinking: Basics, Tools, Cases. Wiley, 2012.

•	Swaiger, Paul C. Digital Transformation: A Guide for Leaders in the Age of Disruption. Harvard Business Review Press, 2017.

•	Thiel, Peter, and Blake Masters. Zero to One: Notes on Startups, or How to Build the Future. Crown Business, 2014.

•	Trott, Paul. Innovation Management and New Product Development. Pearson, 2012.

•	Trout, Jack, and Al Ries. Positioning: The Battle for Your Mind. McGraw-Hill Education,

2000.

• Tushman, M. L., & O'Reilly, C. A. Winning in transitions. Harvard Business School Press. 1997

• Voss, Chris, et al. The Toyota Way to Service Excellence: Lean Transformation in Service Organizations. Productivity Press, 2016.

• Weinberg, Tamar. The Double-Daring Book for Girls. HarperCollins, 2012.

• Weinberg, Gerald M., and Gregory P. Shea. The Real Truth About Success: What the Top 1% Do Differently, Why They Won't Tell You, and How You Can Do It Anyway. Jossey-Bass, 2009.

• Womack, James P., Daniel T. Jones, and Daniel Roos. The Machine That Changed the World: The Story of Lean Production--Toyota's Secret Weapon in the Global Car Wars That Is Now Revolutionizing World Industry. Free Press, 2007.

• Zaltman, Gerald. How Customers Think: Essential Insights into the Mind of the Market. Harvard Business Review Press, 2003.

• Zarrella, Dan. The Social Media Marketing Book. O'Reilly Media, 2009.

• Ziglar, Zig. Secrets of Closing the Sale. Berkley, 2004.

• World Bank. Doing Business reports.

• Ministry of Micro, Small, and Medium Enterprises. Annual Reports. Government of India

www.ingramcontent.com/pod-product-compliance
Lightning Source LLC
LaVergne TN
LVHW011012200726
843509LV00011B/1073
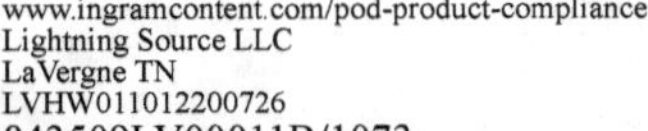